Cambridge Elements ≡

Elements in Epistemology
edited by
Stephen Hetherington
University of New South Wales, Sydney

FOUNDATIONALISM

Richard Fumerton
University of Iowa

CAMBRIDGE
UNIVERSITY PRESS

University Printing House, Cambridge CB2 8BS, United Kingdom

One Liberty Plaza, 20th Floor, New York, NY 10006, USA

477 Williamstown Road, Port Melbourne, VIC 3207, Australia

314–321, 3rd Floor, Plot 3, Splendor Forum, Jasola District Centre, New Delhi – 110025, India

103 Penang Road, #05–06/07, Visioncrest Commercial, Singapore 238467

Cambridge University Press is part of the University of Cambridge.

It furthers the University's mission by disseminating knowledge in the pursuit of education, learning, and research at the highest international levels of excellence.

www.cambridge.org
Information on this title: www.cambridge.org/9781009013949
DOI: 10.1017/9781009028868

© Richard Fumerton 2022

First published 2022

A catalogue record for this publication is available from the British Library.

ISBN 978-1-009-01394-9 Paperback
ISSN 2398-0567 (online)
ISSN 2514-3832 (print)

Foundationalism

Elements in Epistemology

DOI: 10.1017/9781009028868
First published online: June 2022

Richard Fumerton
University of Iowa

Author for correspondence: Richard Fumerton, richard-fumerton@uiowa.edu

Abstract: Foundationalism is a view about the structure of knowledge and justification. The heart of the thesis is the claim that if there is any knowledge or justified belief at all, then there is a kind of knowledge and justified belief that does not require inference from something else known or justifiably believed. This Element begins by exploring abstract arguments for foundationalism and against proposed alternatives. It then explores disagreements among foundationalists about how to understand foundational knowledge and justified belief, what is plausibly included in the foundations, and what is required for legitimate inference from foundations to the rest of what we believe. The author argues for the conclusion that one can combine insights captured by different versions of foundationalism by making a distinction between ideal justification and justification that falls short of that ideal.

Keywords: knowledge, justification, direct acquaintance, internalism and externalism, foundationalism

ISBNs: 9781009013949 (PB), 9781009028868 (OC)
ISSNs: 2398-0567 (online), 2514-3832 (print)

Contents

1 The Structure of Knowledge and Justified Belief

This Element explores questions about the *structure* of knowledge and justified belief. Foundationalism is the view that if there is any knowledge or justified belief then that knowledge or justified belief rests on a "foundation" of knowledge and justified belief that does not depend on *inference* from anything else known or justifiably believed. Foundationalists need to tell us what would make a belief foundationally known or justifiably believed, and which beliefs, if any, should be included in the relevant foundation. Before we address these questions, however, we should begin by saying a bit more about the knowledge and justified belief that are the subject of the foundationalist's claims.

1.1 Knowledge

Epistemology has always been concerned with the nature of knowledge. Some philosophers have argued that discussion of justified belief arrived on the epistemological scene rather late.[1] There is also a great deal of debate over whether it is knowledge or justified belief that is the more *fundamental* epistemological concept. Some think that our understanding of knowledge is parasitic on our understanding of justified belief. Others, those in the "knowledge first" camp, believe precisely the opposite.[2]

Historically, the kind of knowledge that concerns epistemologists is *propositional* knowledge – knowledge *that* such and such is the case, where what is known is the kind of thing that is true or false.[3] But we also talk about knowing places and people, knowing when certain things have happened, knowing why certain things have happened, and knowing how to do certain things. Perhaps one can "translate" talk about knowing places and people into talk of knowing truths. One knows Paris when one knows *that* the Eiffel Tower, the Champs-Elysées, the Cathedral of Notre Dame, and so on are in such and such a place, although one might also insist that the knowledge in question must be in some sense "first hand" (as opposed to knowledge gained through books, for example). Similarly, it seems entirely plausible to suppose that if I know when something happened then I know that it happened at such and such

---

[1] Most notably Plantinga (1992).

[2] The most influential philosopher who holds this view is Williamson (2000).

[3] It is known as propositional knowledge because at least some philosophers identify the kind of thing that is most fundamentally true or false as something they call a proposition. There is much disagreement about what kind of thing a proposition is. The English sentence "The table is brown" (whether true or false) makes the same assertion as the French sentence "La table est brun." We might use the term "proposition" to refer to what is asserted by both sentences (the proposition that the table is brown). Some (although by no means most) would argue that propositions expressed by sentences are thoughts. But this claim raises issues that go far beyond the scope of this Element.

a time, and if I know why something happened, I know that such and such explains it. More controversially, one might suppose that one knows how to play golf when one knows *that* the most effective way to grip a club and hit a ball is such and such. But again, this sort of translation is elusive. I know a lot of people who have extensive propositional knowledge about golf swings and who can't play golf well at all. I also know people who know how to play golf very well and who don't seem to know many truths describing how they are hitting the ball the way they do. It is not tried as often (and it is not really plausible) but one might also entertain the possibility that one can reduce (translate) talk about knowing *that* to talk about knowing *how*. One might assert, for example, that one knows *that* the animal that made the tracks is a deer just insofar as one knows *how* to read those tracks.

We won't try to settle here questions about whether one can identify one sort of knowledge with another. We will simply assume, without argument, that the tradition is correct in thinking that philosophers curious about *truth* are primarily interested in questions concerning propositional knowledge (knowing that . . .).

1.2 Justified (Rational) Belief

It is harder to find historically important philosophers who talked explicitly about the distinction between justified and unjustified belief. In his dialogue *Theatetus*, Plato raised the question of what must be added to true belief in order to get knowledge. The answer he seemed to suggest is often translated as "true belief with an account." It is not clear precisely what he meant, but many twentieth-century philosophers argue that he had in mind something like *justified* true belief.

What is the difference between knowledge and justified belief? One obvious point of contrast is that almost everyone agrees that one can only know that P when P is true.[4] But one can be justified in believing that P (one can rationally believe that P) even if P is false. So if I meet you at a party and you introduce yourself as Harry, most would agree that I would be quite justified in believing (it would be rational for me to believe) that your name is "Harry." And that is so even if it turns out that you are a pathological liar who thinks that it is funny to mislead people with respect to your name. I couldn't *know* that your name is

---

[4] It's not as if people won't sometimes say that they knew something that turned out to be false. The irate bettor who lost the kitchen sink on a horse race might complain: "But I just *knew* Crazylegs was going to win – I don't know what happened." And there is a new movement afoot (Littlejohn, forthcoming, and Williamson, forthcoming) to deny that there *can* be justified false belief. (Although proponents of the view will concede that someone can have a false belief and be "excused" for the mistake.)

"Harry" if it isn't, but I could be justified in believing that that is your name even if it isn't.

We may need to make more distinctions, however, in order to identify the kind of justification or rationality that is of primary interest to the epistemologist. *Epistemic* justification is supposed to have something to do with the likelihood of a belief's being true. If one is epistemically justified in believing that P then one's belief has some feature that makes it likely that what is believed is true (and not by *causing* the world to change in such a way that one's belief is true). By contrast, one might have another sort of reason to believe that P that has nothing to do with its being likely that P is true. I might live with a paralyzing fear that I will die someday, and I might decide that I would be better off all things considered if I could somehow get myself to believe that I am immortal. Or to take another example often used, I might be told that, although I have an illness that will almost certainly kill me, my odds of survival will go up ever so slightly if I can just get myself to believe that I will recover. These considerations might give me *prudential* reasons to believe that I am immortal and to believe that I will recover from my illness even if I don't have the sort of reason that makes likely the truth of what I believe.

Others have argued that one might even have *moral* reasons to believe something that is epistemically irrational to believe. Firth (1959) once argued that one might have a moral reason to believe in one's son's innocence even if there is strong epistemic justification to believe that he is guilty of a crime. One might even be able to imagine a dystopian future in which society tries to make it legally obligatory (and thus create legal reasons) to form certain beliefs.

1.2.1 Epistemic versus Propositional Justification

It is *epistemic* justification with which epistemologists are primarily concerned. But we still need to make one more distinction – the distinction between doxastic and propositional justification. There might be good epistemic reasons for you to believe P even if you don't believe P at all or the cause of your belief has nothing to do with the epistemic reasons available to you for believing P. In such a case, some epistemologists will say that there is *propositional* justification for you to believe P. But we also talk about someone's belief that P having the property of being epistemically justified. On one view, your belief is *doxastically* justified when you believe that P and the belief is *based on* the propositional justification that there is for you to believe that P. And on *one* view about basing, your belief is based on the propositional justification J you have for believing that P when your belief that P is caused (in the right sort of way)[5] by the existence of J. Later in this Element I'll emphasize that the most important sort of epistemic justification that is of concern to philosophers is *propositional* justification.

1.3 Knowledge or Justification – Which, if Either, Is More Fundamental?

You will recall that some epistemologists suggested that we should try to understand knowledge as (doxastically) justified true belief. Almost everyone these days agrees that even if knowledge is *partially* constituted by justified true belief, one needs to add some further condition. Although Russell gave examples that made a similar point, Gettier (1963) most clearly illustrated the problem with identifying knowledge as nothing more than justified true belief. He asked you to imagine various situations in which you will realize that someone has a justified true belief but doesn't have knowledge. Consider an example from Russell (1949, 170–71). Suppose you reach a conclusion about the time by looking at a clock that (unbeknownst to you) is broken. As the old saying goes, even a broken clock tells the right time twice a day, and if you get lucky you might form not only a justified, but also a true belief about the time by looking at the clock. But this sort of "lucky" true belief doesn't count as knowledge, does it?

Among those convinced that they were still on the right track with their justified-true-belief account of knowledge, the search began for additional conditions that would get us the right result. Entire books have been written evaluating various proposals, and it is an understatement to suggest that the additional requirements for knowledge have been elusive. Convinced that the search is futile, Williamson (2000) argued in his highly influential work *Knowledge: Its Scope and its Limits* that one should give up the attempt to break down knowledge into constituent parts, one of which was doxastically justified belief. Rather, he suggested, we should reverse course, and try to understand justified belief in terms of an unanalyzed concept of knowledge. Put crudely, the idea is that a justified belief is a belief supported by evidence, where one's evidence should be identified with what one knows.

---

[5] Causal theories of just about anything always face the problem of *deviant* causal chains. I could probably conjure up some really roundabout way in which the fact that you have propositional justification for believing that P causes you to believe that P, but you won't think of the belief as *based* on that justification. The existence of the justification might, for example, cause a hypnotist at the party to worry that you haven't formed a belief based on that justification, which, in turn, causes the hypnotist to use hypnosis to get you to form the relevant belief.

While I can't defend the view here, I count myself as among those who think that the concept of justified belief is more fundamental than the concept of knowledge. The foundationalist's thesis can be stated as either a claim about knowledge or as a claim about justified belief. In what follows, I'll talk mainly about justified belief, although most of what I say about justification will apply *mutatis mutandis* to knowledge. I'll also try to make clear that there are views about the foundations of justification that are hospitable to the idea that the foundations of justification are identical with foundational knowledge.

1.4 The Distinction between Inferential and Noninferential Justification; Inferential and Noninferential Knowledge

Foundationalism is a view about the *structure* of justification and knowledge. It seems almost obvious to many that the justification we have for some of our beliefs depends on our having other *different* justified beliefs. Put another way, it seems obvious to many that much of our justification is *inferential*. I justifiably believe that a newspaper reported that there was an earthquake this morning in California, and from this (and perhaps my justified belief that the newspaper is reliable) I *infer* that the earthquake took place. Notice that getting a justified belief through inference of this sort does require that I have *justified* beliefs about the paper. The epistemological slogan – garbage in; garbage out – seems right. I can't get justified beliefs about the evil deeds of world leaders if I base those beliefs solely on outlandish, wildly irrational conspiracy theories.

Just as justification for a belief might involve inference, so also might knowledge. Indeed, if I *know* what the headlines of the paper are and that the paper is highly reliable, you might think that through legitimate inference I can acquire *knowledge* that the earthquake rocked California. But again I couldn't get knowledge that C when my sole reason for believing C was E unless I know that E – no knowledge in; no knowledge out.

If we have the ideas of inferential justification and knowledge, we can define negatively the ideas of noninferential justification and knowledge. Noninferential justification for believing P is justification for believing P that is *not* inferential. Noninferential knowledge is knowledge that is *not* inferential. Philosophers who believe that there is noninferential knowledge will also sometimes refer to that knowledge as *direct*, and refer to what is known as that which is *self-evident*. As we will see later, the concept of what is known directly is also sometimes associated with the idea of some aspect of reality simply being *given* to one.

1.5 Regress Arguments for Foundationalism

Although I can't argue for this here, I do think that in the history of philosophy almost all philosophers just took for granted that some version of foundationalism is true. But the most famous of the *arguments* for foundationalism are regress arguments. In the opening paragraph of this Element, I characterized foundationalism about justification and knowledge by employing a *conditional*: *If* there is any knowledge and *if* there are any justified beliefs, *then* there is noninferential knowledge and there are noninferentially justified beliefs. With the ideas of inferential knowledge and justification, we can state these views about justification and knowledge in a slightly different way:

The Conditional Foundationalist Claim about Justification: If there are any justified beliefs then those beliefs are either noninferentially justified beliefs or they are beliefs involving inferences that can be traced back ultimately to beliefs that are noninferentially justified (the *foundations* of justification).

The Conditional Foundationalist Claim about Knowledge: If there is any knowledge then that knowledge is either noninferential knowledge or it is knowledge that involves inferences that can be traced back ultimately to knowledge that is noninferential.

While the conditional claims are accepted by all foundationalists, *almost all* foundationalists also accept the *unconditional* claims that there are justified beliefs and there is knowledge. That together with the conditional claims entail that there are noninferentially justified beliefs and there is noninferential knowledge. The most well-known regress argument for foundationalism, the *epistemic* regress argument, takes it to be obvious that there are justified beliefs and that there is knowledge. In what follows, I'll talk mainly about the structure of justification, but exactly analogous arguments would apply to the structure of knowledge.

1.5.1 The Epistemic Regress Argument for Foundationalism

We have already had occasion to note that the foundationalist takes it to be obvious that J) Someone S acquires justification for believing P by inferring P from something else E, only if that person S is justified in believing E. Some foundationalists also believe that IJ) S acquires justification for believing P by inferring P from E only if S has some sort of access to the fact that E (at the very least) makes *probable* that P.

The epistemic regress argument relying on J) goes as follows:

1) If all justification were inferential, then, given J, S justifiably believes P only if S infers P from something else E1 that S justifiably believes. But if all

justification were inferential then S justifiably believes E1 only if S infers E1 from yet another proposition E2 that S justifiably believes, a proposition that would need to be inferred from still another proposition E3 that S justifiably believes . . ., and so on, ad infinitum.

2) From 1) it follows that to justifiably believe any proposition P S would need to complete infinitely many inferences, and *that* no finite being can do.

3) There are justified beliefs.

Therefore,

4) Not all justified beliefs are inferentially justified – there are noninferentially justified beliefs that ground all inferentially justified beliefs.

If one also thinks that IJ) is true, and that access to E's making probable P involves justifiably believing that E makes probable P,[6] the thesis that all justification is inferential would require one to complete not only one but infinitely many infinitely long chains of reasoning to have a justified belief. To justifiably believe that P one would need to infer P from E1 *and* infer that E1 makes probable P. This last claim one would need to infer from some other proposition F1 that one justifiably believes on the basis of some other proposition F2 that one infers from . . ., and so on ad infinitum. But one would also need to justifiably believe that F1 does makes likely that E1 makes likely P, something that one would need to infer from G1 that one would need to infer from G2 . . . and so on. And one would also need to infer that G2 makes likely that G1 makes likely that E1 makes likely P, and . . .. The regresses are generated in infinitely many directions.

It is worth emphasizing that to get the conclusion that there actually *are* noninferentially justified beliefs one needs the premise that there *are* justified beliefs. Without that premise, one is left choosing between the existence of foundational justification and the most radical form of skepticism – the view that we have no justification for believing anything at all. This radical form of skepticism is often rejected as epistemically *self-refuting* in that it entails that no one could justifiably believe *it*. It is not clear, however, that a skeptic this extreme would be fazed by this charge. The skeptic might put the argument out there and tell you that the ball is now in your court. If you don't like the conclusion, figure out what is wrong with the argument. If forced to choose between accepting this extreme skepticism and embracing foundationalism, however, almost all philosophers will do the latter.[7]

---

[6] We'll talk later about whether we can construe the access in question in some other way.

[7] Although I'm not suggesting that all foundationalists embrace their view *because* they want to avoid skepticism.

1.5.2 The Conceptual Regress Argument

As I will suggest later, the *conceptual* regress argument for foundationalism might be stronger than the epistemic regress argument. In short, the conceptual regress argument purports to establish that the very *idea* of epistemic justification is built on the *idea* of noninferential justification. The argument relies again on that distinction we drew earlier between inferential and noninferential justification. We have the idea of a justified belief and the idea that *one* way a belief might be justified is through inference. But if we try to explain the idea of inferential justification for believing P in terms of the idea of a legitimate inference from some other proposition *justifiably* believed, our account hasn't yet explained the more general concept of a justified belief. Our account of inferential justification presupposes an understanding of justified belief. Put another way, when we think only about inferential justification, we haven't yet located in thought the *source* of justification.

Consider an analogy. One of the earliest distinctions made in ethics is the distinction between different ways in which something can be good. Some things, like taking blood-pressure medication, are good only as a *means* to something else that is good (perhaps health or the happiness that comes from being in good health). But, one might argue, it can't be the case that *everything* that is good is good only as *means* to something else that is good. While we can (partially) define being good *as a means* in terms of having good outcomes, we can't *complete* our definition of goodness this way. To find, even in thought, the *source* of goodness, we need to form the thought of something that is good *in itself* (intrinsically good, good just in virtue of what it is).

The suggestion here is that inferential justification stands to noninferential justification as being good as a means stands to being good in itself. Put more formally, many foundationalists explicitly or implicitly adopt a *recursive* analysis of justification. The basic idea of a recursive analysis is relatively straightforward. We have, for example, the idea of being a descendant of someone. What is that idea? Well, it clearly has something to do with the idea of being a child of someone. Am I the descendant of X just when I am the child of X? No. I might be the child of a child of X, or the child of a child of a child of X, and so on. We understand the "and so on" (we understand the recursion) and so we grasp the concept of being a descendant. We build that recursive idea on the *base* clause (the conceptual building block) of being a child of someone.

Just as one can recursively define the concept of being a descendant of S relying on the idea of being a child of X, so also one might argue that one can recursively define being good in terms of the "base clause" of being good in itself. To be good is to be good in itself, *or* to be something that brings about something that is good in itself, or to be something that brings about something that brings about something that is good in itself . . ., and so on. Analogously, the *foundationalist* in epistemology might argue that we can define justified belief as belief that is either noninferentially justified, *or* is inferred legitimately from some proposition that is noninferentially justified, *or* is inferred legitimately from some proposition that is inferred legitimately from something that is noninferentially justified, and so on. On this view, we need the idea of non-inferential (foundational) justification to form the idea of justification. The idea of being noninferentially justified in believing something is the conceptual building block on which we build the idea of justified belief.

1.6 A Foundationalist "Argument" for Foundationalism

The regress arguments for foundationalism are abstract arguments. As we shall see, their premises have been challenged by those who reject foundationalism. There is a more blunt reason for embracing foundationalism, one that its critics are likely to reject as question begging. If foundationalism *is* a correct account of justification, and there *are* noninferentially justified beliefs, there would be no reason in principle why foundationalists might not claim that we have noninferentially justified beliefs that foundationalism is true – we have non-inferentially justified beliefs that we have noninferentially justified beliefs (at least once we possess the concept of having a noninferentially justified belief).[8] Indeed, I would argue that this is precisely the attitude that many seventeenth- and eighteenth-century epistemologists implicitly had. When you stub your toe and experience that familiar searing pain, ask yourself what *evidence* you have for believing that you are in pain. From what do you *infer* that you are in pain? The question invites an incredulous stare. You don't *need* to infer that you are in pain when you are immediately aware of the pain. The pain is simply *there* before your consciousness.[9] Something like this, I will argue, is precisely right. But here, I'm just pointing to the oddity of supposing that you *infer* that you are in pain from something else that you believe.

Or consider a quite different example. Euclid developed an impressive geometry, one that rests on axioms for which he didn't argue. If a precocious student of Euclid demanded an argument for the axioms before agreeing to reach any conclusions based on those axioms, Euclid would presumably have impatiently answered that we don't need a proof to "see" that the axioms are

---

[8] It may be that it requires a fair bit of philosophical sophistication to acquire the idea of a noninferentially justified belief.

[9] And contrast this with our judgment about another person's being in pain. We do infer the pain of another from truths about how they are behaving (including their verbal behavior).

true. If we think clearly about the axioms, their truth will simply be evident to us.

Again, I'm not suggesting that the foundationlist's critics will be moved by these appeals to the alleged fact that we have, without any sort of inference, justified belief in (and knowledge of) these truths. One who doesn't think that there is noninferential justification won't be impressed by an assertion that we have noninferential justification for believing that the foundations exist! But neither should the foundationalist be seduced into conceding that the only justification one could have for thinking that there are noninferentially justified beliefs is justification that requires a legitimate inference from other truths justifiably believed. Foundationalists should not apologize for being foundationalists.

1.7 Alternatives to Foundationalism and the Foundationalist's Responses

Foundationalism has its critics. Some don't understand what could possibly justify a belief but another belief. It is difficult to assess such claims until one has a positive account of what would make knowledge or justified belief noninferential, and we haven't done more than hint at such an account yet. The most we can do here is critically evaluate alternative views, views that reject one or more of the premises of the foundationalist's arguments.

1.7.1 The Coherence Theory of Justification

One of the most historically significant alternatives to foundationalism is the coherence theory of justification. Convinced that there is no escaping the "circle of beliefs," the coherentist rejects the foundationalist's presupposition that it is only an *already* justified belief that can give support to other beliefs one has. The basic idea, as the name of the theory implies, is that a given belief enjoys justification when it *coheres* (in the right sort of way) with other beliefs. Proponents of the view sometimes explain their view by suggesting that they reject the foundationalist's presupposition that justification is *linear* – the idea that to be justified in believing P through inference one needs *first* to be justified in believing some proposition other than P. Instead, we should think that we form beliefs in order to complete a nice, clear "picture" of reality, the way a successfully completed jigsaw puzzle gives us a nice picture of something. Each belief contributes to our representation of reality, the way the placement of each piece in the puzzle contributes to the completion of the puzzle's picture.

Coherence theorists need to tell us how they understand coherence, and what they think a belief must cohere *with* to enjoy the status of justified belief.

Probably the most common sort of coherence theory of justification views the justification of a given person's belief as a function of the way that belief coheres with the rest of what *that person* believes. But one might also try to understand justification in terms of the way a person's belief coheres with the rest of the beliefs of that person's community, or even the way in which a person's belief coheres with the beliefs an *ideal* believer would have. But if one starts talking about ideal believers one better not identify the ideal believer with a person who forms *rational* beliefs. At least one better not do that if one wants to avoid the appearance of problematic circularity in one's account of epistemically rational beliefs.

A coherence theory of justification is distinct from a coherence theory of truth. The latter tries to understand truth itself in terms of the coherence of beliefs. A coherence theorist of truth would presumably need to relativize truth to a belief system and reject as ill formed the idea of something's being true or false *simpliciter*. It is an understatement to suggest that a coherence theory of truth is a pill too bitter for most philosophers to swallow.

Foundationalists will object to the coherence theory of justification in a number of ways. One sort of objection employs relatively straightforward thought experiments. Earlier, we appealed to the idea that one doesn't get justified beliefs by inferring conclusions from premises that one would be wildly irrational to accept. We should also worry about this sort of scenario when evaluating a coherence theory of justification. Paranoid schizophrenics often have fascinatingly intricate webs of interlocking beliefs. But most of us are convinced that they don't get themselves *justified* beliefs by weaving tapestries of thoughts pulled out of thin air.

We have noted already that the coherence theorist needs some sort of account of what makes one belief cohere with others. Almost all coherence theorists assume that coherence would *minimally* involve consistency. One doesn't have a coherent system of beliefs when all of one's beliefs cannot possibly be true together. Taking that for granted, coherence theorists worry that *mere* consistency isn't enough and that other sorts of mutual support would be required for justified belief.[10] But Foley (1979) pointed out that internal consistency among one's beliefs might not even be *necessary* for a belief in one's set of beliefs to be justified. Consider the well-known preface paradox. Most of us who write books try to carefully check the final proofs for typographical errors before we OK the proofs for publication. But some of us also take care to write in our prefaces that we are quite sure that the book contains errors *somewhere*. Those who write this in their preface also might

---

[10] See, for example, BonJour (1985).

believe that there are no errors on page 1, on page 2, on page 3, and so on, even as they are confident that some page or other contains errors. Lotteries are like this as well. A rational person will believe of each ticket that it is a loser even as he or she is confident that *some* ticket will win.[11] These beliefs taken together cannot all be true. So internal consistency of what one believes doesn't seem to be even necessary for justification.

A related problem involves belief in propositions that are necessarily false. Trivially, a necessary falsehood (like $2 + 2 = 5$) cannot be true. It is a hazard of fields such as philosophy and mathematics that we sometimes end up believing something to be true that is, in fact, *necessarily* false (although, of course, the fact that it is necessarily false might be *very* difficult to discern). If I believe that P when P is necessarily false, then the totality of my beliefs must contain a falsehood. Yet it seems absurd to suppose that one belief in a necessary falsehood will preclude *all* of the rest of my beliefs from being justified (see Fumerton 1994).

Another now well-known objection to a coherence theory of justification involves the plausible idea that however we understand coherence, coherence without *awareness* of coherence doesn't seem to bring with it anything that can be plausibly construed as justification.[12] Suppose I randomly come to believe a complex set of propositions that do, in fact, cohere wonderfully. But I don't have the mental acuity to *recognize* the fact that the beliefs do cohere in this way. Could the mere coherence do me any good by way of giving me justified beliefs? If we answer that it cannot, and we try to revise our coherence theory by requiring that we have some sort of epistemic access to coherence in order to get justification, one needs an answer to the question of how to understand this talk of *access* to coherence. We have already decided that coherence by itself won't do the work, so won't we be forced to leave the confines of our coherence theory of justification? Won't we need to suppose that we have direct access to (justified beliefs about) what we believe and the fact that our beliefs cohere?

1.7.2 Foundherentism

Haack (1995) and Chisholm (1989, chapter 7), among others, explored combining alleged insights of both foundationalism and coherentism into a *hybrid*

---

[11] One might argue that if one really believed that the ticket one was thinking of purchasing was a loser, one wouldn't buy it. But it seems to me that the decision is analogous to buying flight insurance. I don't believe that my plane is about to crash, but if the cost of the insurance is minimal, I might still protect against that possibility. See also Hawthorne (2003).

[12] Ironically, perhaps, it was BonJour (1985), when he defended a coherence theory of justification, who did as much as anyone to make clear this problem faced by a coherence theorist.

view, a view that Haack dubbed "foundherentism."[13] The basic idea here is that there are noninferentially justified beliefs, and that all justified beliefs owe their justification *in part* to foundations on which they are built. *But* beliefs can get additional justification in virtue of the fact that they cohere with each other. I can't do justice to the view here, but I have at least two concerns. First, it is not clear to me what *need* there would be for coherence. Suppose that E1 by itself justifies to some extent my belief that P, and E2 justifies to some extent my belief that Q, and, further, that P and Q cohere in a way that is supposed to enhance the justification I have for believing each. Why shouldn't we just conclude that the complex (E1 and E2) provides stronger justification for believing P, and for believing Q? Why do we need to appeal to the notion of coherence?[14]

Furthermore, worries about the coherence theory of justification will emerge again when we turn to the epistemic role coherence is supposed to play by way of enhancing justification. It still seems possible to have jointly inconsistent but individually justified beliefs, and coherence without access to coherence still seems epistemically impotent.

1.7.3 Infinitism

Peter Klein's (1998) infinitist view of justification is a relatively late entry into the list of epistemological accounts of justified belief. Convinced that there is no plausible, nonarbitrary way of ending the need for inference to justify belief, Klein rejects the foundationalist's view that there would *need* to be such an end in order for there to be justified beliefs. The rough idea behind his view is that one is justified in believing C when one has the *capacity* to come up with an argument for C. Klein agrees with the foundationalist that one would also need to have justification for believing the premises of *that* argument, call them P1, and he argues that one would have that justification provided that one has the *capacity* to come up with another different argument (with different premises) for P1, and so on, ad infinitum. Unlike the foundationalist, the infinitist doesn't

---

[13] Chisholm called the feature of a belief system that can add to foundational justification *concurrence*. Haack used the metaphor of a crossword puzzle to explain her view. The clues give one some reason to think that one has found the right word to enter in the puzzle. But when that word "fits" with the other words one comes up with in response to additional clues, one gets more support for one's initial answer.

[14] Mike Huemer pointed out to me that one might still appeal to the relevance of coherence at the *foundational* level. If there can be noninferentially justified false beliefs, I might have a noninferentially justified belief that E1 and a noninferentially justified belief that E2, where these beliefs also mutually support each other. I think what one should say in such a situation is that one can simultaneously have noninferential justification for believing each proposition while each belief also enjoys inferential justification.

see why the need for infinitely many capacities of this sort is an insuperable obstacle to our having justified beliefs.

Philosophers often distinguish between conscious (occurrent beliefs) and dispositional beliefs.[15] As you read this Element, I could truly describe you as believing that $2 > 1$, that $3 > 1$, that $4 > 1$, and so on. You probably weren't thinking of these truths before you read the previous sentence, but, in *some* sense, you did have those beliefs. You not only have infinitely many beliefs of this sort, but all of them are presumably justified. So it seems that a finite being *can* have infinitely many justified beliefs, and the foundationalist should be cautious in making general claims about the limitations of finite beings when it comes to "containing" infinitudes of this sort.[16]

There is much that can be said by way of evaluating infinitism. The view is surprisingly resilient to some of the first objections that come to mind. To my way of thinking, however, the view doesn't have the resources to respond to the *conceptual* regress argument for foundationalism. At least that is so if the infinitist purports to be offering an account of what makes a belief justified. As you will recall, one doesn't get justification for believing some conclusion C by inferring it from some premise P1 unless one has justification for believing P1. The infinitist's view just isn't plausible if all it requires for justified belief is the capacity to present arguments for everything one believes. That's just too easy. Suppose that I believe that there are zebra in my basement. You want an argument for what I believe. Here it is: 1) All of my beliefs about zebra are true, and 2) I believe that there are zebra in the basement, so 3) There are zebra in my basement. You want an argument for premises 1) and 2)? Here it is: 3) All of my second-order beliefs (beliefs about first-order beliefs) are true and 4) I have second-order beliefs about 1) and 2), and so 5) 1) and 2) are true. You want an argument for 3) and 4): All of my third-order beliefs (beliefs about second-order beliefs) are true and . . .. You get the idea. Of course, we don't think that this rather superficial skill at constructing valid arguments actually does me any good when it comes to getting justification for believing that there are zebra in my basement, because you realize that I need not only beliefs, but *justified* beliefs in the premises of these infinitely many arguments.

---

[15] The distinction is not easy to define. Dispositional beliefs, or, perhaps better, subconscious beliefs, are not just dispositions to believe something. You might be the kind of person who would believe *for the first time* that there is life on other planets if you were to consider the question. But that doesn't make it true that there is any sense in which you had that belief before you considered the questions. There are other technical problems with trying to define dispositional beliefs using conditionals. See Shope (1978).

[16] Arguably, we possess other capacities to perform infinitely many tasks. It seems that there are infinitely many grammatical sentences each of which I could form (although perhaps I couldn't utter all of them) – "I am over 1" tall," "I am over 1 and ½" tall," "I am over 1 and ¼" tall," and so on. See Huemer (2019) for an argument that finite minds cannot have infinitely many beliefs.

But now our entire account of justified belief rests on an unanalyzed (unexplained) concept of justification.[17]

2 What *Could* Make a Belief Noninferentially Justified?

It is one thing to convince oneself that there must be foundationally justified beliefs if there are any justified beliefs; there must be foundational knowledge if there is to be any knowledge. It is quite another to come up with a plausible account of what *constitutes* foundational justification or knowledge.

2.1 Nonstarters: "Explanations" that Don't Explain

One way to start thinking about how to understand foundations is to carefully consider what one takes to be the best candidates for inclusion in our foundations. Earlier we talked about the bewilderment one might feel if pressed to identify the evidence from which one *infers* that one is in searing pain, or the frustration Euclid might feel if we insist that he provide arguments for the most fundamental axioms of his geometry. When asked what justifies you in believing that you are in pain, you might respond with emphasis: "The fact that I *am* in pain." When asked what justifies you in believing some axiomatic truth, P, you might respond with emphasis: "The fact that P *is* true." But neither response offers even a hint as to what it is about your *relation* to the fact that you are in pain, or the fact that P, that distinguishes your epistemic situation to these facts from any other features of the world. You wouldn't be much impressed if I argued for theism by stating with emphasis that I know that there is a God because there *is* a God. Neither would you be impressed if I claim to know that I have a cancerous tumor in my brain because there *is* one.

The moral seems to me that it must be something about my *relation* to pain and my *relation* to whatever makes Euclid's axioms true that accounts for the special sort of justification I have for the respective beliefs.[18] Even those who talk of certain truths being self-evident are implicitly acknowledging, I would

---

[17] In response to Fumerton (2014), Klein (2014) responds that he wasn't trying to *define* epistemic justification. Rather, he thought of infinitism as only a view about the *structure* of justification. The views I am discussing in this Element, however, are attempts to say what makes a belief justified.

[18] I continue to use as a paradigm of truths that might be known directly the axioms of Euclidean geometry. I know full well that there are alleged to be alternatives to Euclidean geometry, and that some would even argue that we have "discovered" that Euclidean geometry isn't actually true. This is a "hit and run" comment, but I'll just assert here that no one has discovered that Euclidean geometry is false. The most anyone might truly assert is that few, if any, bodies travel in Euclidean straight lines (and thus for describing the behavior of some sorts of micro-entities, Euclidean geometry might not be very useful). Haven't we learned, however, that space itself is non-Euclidean? No.

suggest, that the truth, or what makes the truth true, are *presented* to one in a way that creates a special sort of justification or knowledge.

2.2 The Internalism/Externalism Controversy

Due largely to the work of Alvin Goldman, the field of epistemology has split into two camps, those who embrace some version of *internalism* and those who embrace some version of *externalism*.[19] Both internalists and externalists are often (although not always) foundationalists. They differ dramatically, however, on how they understand foundational justification. This isn't a work in the history of philosophy, so I won't try to argue for the following claim, but I do think that in the history of philosophy the vast majority of those interested in epistemology *implicitly* accepted some form of internalism.[20]

It is not easy to define the internalism/externalism controversy. I'll talk briefly about *inferential* justification towards the end of this Element, but for now I'll focus on a debate over the nature of foundational justification (and whatever else would turn a noninferentially justified true belief into foundational knowledge).[21]

There are two main versions of internalism. The first (suggested by the label) is the view that all justification, including, therefore, foundational justification (assuming there is such), is solely constituted by the internal states of a believer — let's call this *internal-state internalism*. For our purposes, we will say that a state of S is internal to S if it is a feature of S that requires the existence of no other conscious being or any other *physical* object. So, on my view, pains, sensations, thoughts, awareness of my pains, awareness of numbers and sensations, all count as internal states.[22]

A second sort of internalism (*access* internalism) centers on the claim that the only thing that could possibly justify me in believing something is some feature

---

[19] I don't want to get involved in an argument about who the "first" externalists were. Quine certainly had an influence, but I think that Goldman was the clearest and most influential of the externalists.

[20] It's complicated and these days externalists will often try to find "proto" externalists among those I take to be internalists.

[21] If there can be noninferentially justified false beliefs, then for a noninferentially justified belief to be knowledge it would also need to be true. But even that might not be enough. Once we allow that a justified belief *can* be false, it seems easy enough to imagine a justified true belief that is true through sheer luck. Lucky true belief doesn't seem to be knowledge. It is, however, very hard to define the relevant notion of luck.

[22] I emphasize on *my* view. There is another internalism/externalism controversy about how to understand mental states. Externalists about the content of mind argue that at least some internal states have the content they do (are about what they are about) only in virtue of being the end product of a causal chain that goes all the way back to the kind of object that the thought is about. There is no necessary connection between an externalist in epistemology and being an externalist about the content of mental states.

to which I have, or could have, introspective access. As a first stab, introspection is the relation one has to certain of one's states when one "looks inside" and pays attention to the character of one's experience (but I'll talk more about how best to understand introspection later). The two versions of internalism have a possible (albeit not unproblematic) connection. The British empiricists (among others) took our internal states to be exhausted by mental states, and some took it to be the *mark* of the mental that it is introspectively accessible.[23]

For our purposes, I'll simply define two versions of externalism in terms of the *rejection* of internalism. So we have *access* externalists and externalists who think that justification (at least often) depends on facts that go *beyond* the present internal states of believers.

2.3 Internalist Versions of Foundationalism

2.3.1 Direct Acquaintance

While it may not be the most popular internalist account of foundational justification, I'll nevertheless start with the view that I take to be correct.[24] In thinking about the justification I have for believing that I am now in pain, I asked above how I am *related* to pain in such a way as to obviate the need for evidence from which I need to infer that I'm in pain. Russell, most famously, but many others as well, have suggested that we are directly aware of, or are directly acquainted with the fact of being in pain, the very fact that makes true my belief that I am in pain. The pain is simply "there" before consciousness (or at least it is when one is not distracted), and when one is acquainted with the pain in this way *as* one forms the thought that one is in pain *and* one is acquainted with the fact that the pain makes true the thought, one has noninferential justification for believing that one is in pain, and, I would argue, direct knowledge that one is in pain.[25]

Notice I did not suggest that direct acquaintance with the pain *by itself* gets one knowledge or justified belief. Pain is not the kind of thing that can be true or false. To give an account of direct knowledge or noninferentially justified belief, we need to bring into the story something that can be true or false. On my view, it is *thought* that is the primary bearer of truth value. Beliefs are a *species* of thought, so beliefs can be true or false.[26] Sentences of a language contingently

---

[23] So my blood pressure, for example, might be, in some sense, an internal state of my body, but it wouldn't count as an internal mental state.

[24] That way you will have the true view even if you don't finish reading the rest of the Element!

[25] As Paul Moser once suggested, to be, perhaps, we also need to insist that for knowledge, the relevant belief needs to be based on the noninferential justification in one's possession.

[26] There are other species of thought. Imagining, fearing, desiring, hoping, and seeming to remember all involve thinking of the world's being a certain way. We don't usually talk of

express thoughts and when the thought a sentence expresses is true or false, we can also talk derivatively of the sentence's being true or false. One doesn't need to embrace the view that thoughts are the primary "bearers" of truth and falsehood (truth value) to accept the framework suggested above. We earlier introduced "proposition" as a kind of place holder for *whatever* the primary bearer of truth value is. And as long as one accepts within one's metaphysics (one's view about what kinds of thing exist) propositions as entities with which one can be directly aware, *and* one accepts the intuitively plausible idea that features of the world (facts) are what make representations of the world true, one can embrace the acquaintance theory of noninferential justification.

Again, the idea is that when one has the thought that P as one is directly acquainted with the fact that P and the fact that the fact that P makes true the thought that P, one has noninferential justification for believing that, and one directly knows that P. I haven't said much of anything yet about what kinds of thing might be the objects of direct acquaintance, so I haven't said much of anything yet about what the foundations of knowledge and justified belief include.

The view sketched here raises all sorts of critical philosophical question. What is this relation of direct acquaintance/awareness? What are thoughts? What are facts? And what is this truth-making relation that is supposed to hold between certain facts and the thoughts they make true? (Philosophers who talk this way often embrace what is called the correspondence theory of truth. True propositions *correspond* to features of the world they represent. False propositions don't.)[27]

These are the questions. What are the answers? Well, they might be disappointing. On the view I defend, for example, one can't *define* direct acquaintance, thought, or correspondence. One *can* define a simple fact (also sometimes called an *atomic* fact) as something's exemplifying a property or standing in a relation to another thing, but that will take us to a host of important metaphysical questions about properties, relations, and their exemplification (the question of what is involved in something's having a property or standing in a relation to another thing).[28] It is important to remember that on most views about the nature of philosophy, the attempt to analyze or define interesting philosophical concepts or ideas cannot continue forever. We talked about regress arguments that purport to establish that we need to understand certain

---

a false imagining, a false fear, or a false hope, but we do make a distinction between imagining what isn't the case, or fearing what isn't the case, or hoping for what isn't the case.

[27]   And a whole lot more needs to be said about truth. See Fumerton (2002).

[28]   We'll also need an account of how complex facts (like the fact that Lincoln was a U.S. president and Grant was a U.S. president) are "built" out of simple facts.

ideas in terms of others. But that would only be possible, arguably, if there were ultimately simple ideas, conceptual "atoms," ideas out of which we can build other ideas. Philosophers sometimes make mistakes because they come up with incorrect analyses of various concepts, but they also sometimes make mistakes because they try to analyze the unanalyzable.[29]

If we can't define acquaintance in any interesting way, is there some other way in which we can direct our attention to the relation on which this version of foundationalism is built? Well, we are all familiar with "ostensive" definition. Big Bird on Sesame Street may have enabled you to figure out what having a certain color or shape involves. And he (or she?) did it by giving you examples of a number of things that have the color or shape hoping that you would eventually "clue in." Can we similarly point to the relation of direct acquaintance? I think one can. It is the relation you have to pain, but don't have to high blood pressure, the relation you have to what you are now imagining that you don't have to what I am now imagining, the relation you have to red's being darker than pink, a relation you don't have to the fact that pain is caused by certain neurons firing in the brain.

Not so fast, the critic will complain. I know what it is like to feel pain, to imagine a shape, to experience a color, to think about the relation of being darker than that holds between red and pink, but I don't know what this acquaintance is supposed to be. What is direct awareness of pain, for example, over and above the pain? It is not as if there could be the one without the other.

There are at least two responses. First, it seems almost obvious, at least on reflection, that we are constantly *bombarded* with experiences many of which we don't notice – experiences of which we are unaware. To take a familiar example, we are sometimes surprised when a background noise suddenly stops. It is only when it stops that we have the vague sense that something is different and we will, perhaps, notice when the sound starts up again. Arguably, it involves the exercise of a certain kind of skill to pay close attention to subtle changes in the character of, say, visual experiences. Artists can develop that skill, and, because they possess it, some are able to represent well in their art the differences in colors caused by changes in light and shadow. Most children don't notice the changes in appearance caused by changes in perspective – the way in which visual experience is in *constant* flux as one's relation to the world around one changes.[30] That's why only their loving parents will ever display their "art."

---

[29] Moore (1903) famously claimed that one of the most fundamental mistakes philosophers in ethics make is supposing that one can define what he took to be the indefinable concept of being good in itself.

[30] The changes don't necessarily involve relations to external objects. The experiences of a realistic dream change just the way experiences of waking life change.

Those skeptical about the existence of acquaintance are likely to acknowledge at least some of the alleged data to which I appeal above, but they might
argue that it reflects only the distinction between *having* an experience, and
knowing or justifiably *believing* various propositions describing the character of
that experience (Sosa and BonJour 2003) But if we are trying to explain
foundationally justified belief and knowledge in terms of direct acquaintance,
we had better not in turn explain the relevant acquaintance in terms of justified
belief or knowledge!

Consider again our paradigm of a sensation to which *I* think we have direct
acquaintance, pain. Now imagine a familiar enough situation. I have a bad back
and have been in serious pain most of the day. You visit me and we begin a really
interesting conversation. During that conversation, I go for a period of time
unaware of the pain. When the conservation ends, I notice the pain again.
I suggest that it is at least *possible* that when the pain bothered me it was
a pain of which I was aware, and when the conversation started, the awareness
temporarily ceased. We have isolated in thought direct awareness!

The above argument is far from decisive. Some will argue that the example of
pain described is one in which pain simply *ceases* for a while. The conversation
acts the way hydrocodone acts. It temporarily stops pain. Alternatively, one may
admit that the pain might continue for a while without my noticing it, but this
phenomenon is still best understood in terms of a pain about which one stopped
having *knowledge* or *belief.* But doesn't it at least make *sense* to suppose that
pain can continue without awareness of it, just as some other experience that one
doesn't even have the capacity to represent in thought might continue without
awareness of it? And if it does make sense, I can still get you to attend to direct
acquaintance through the relevant thought experiment.[31]

If you don't like the example of pain, you might also again think about that
background noise discussed earlier, a noise that suddenly stops.[32] When it stops,
one often notices *for the first time* that the auditory sensation was in the
background. That noticing is again the kind of relation to one's experience on
which the acquaintance theorist is relying in giving an account of foundational
knowledge.

Most of our attention has been focused so far on the nature of foundational
knowledge of, and foundational justification for believing, truths about experience. But when we first gave examples of truths that might be known directly,

---

[31] If you don't like the example of pain, think of the vast array of sensations with which we are
constantly bombarded. Surely we are not conscious of all these experiences. But what is the
difference between a conscious experience and an unconscious experience other than the fact
that we are aware of the former?

[32] Huemer suggested to me that this example is more persuasive than the example of pain.

we included the axioms of systems such as geometry, arithmetic, and logic – *necessary* truths. If we are to give a *unified* acquaintance theory of foundational justification and knowledge, we will need to convince ourselves that one can be directly acquainted with the truth-makers for *these* sorts of truth. Unfortunately, to accomplish this goal we would need to settle questions that take us far beyond the scope of this Element. We would need to figure out what the truth-makers are for necessary truths, and we would need to figure out what our relationship is, or could be, to those truth-makers. Here, I'll just sketch two possibilities.

On one view, necessary truths are made true by relations that hold between properties. But there are all sorts of different views about the nature of properties. Some philosophers take properties to be *universals*. When two different things, x and y, are both, say, round, the proponent of the view that there are universals thinks that there is this entity, *roundness*, that is common to both x and y. Of the philosophers who believe this, some take universals to be the kind of thing that can exist even if nothing *has* the property (nothing exemplifies the property); others think that in order for a property to exist, something (now, in the past, or in the future) has to have the property. If you think that there are properties of this sort, you might also think that one can somehow hold such properties before your consciousness. And if you are an acquaintance theorist, you would be comfortable restating that idea in terms of direct awareness of the properties.

As I indicated, those who think that there are properties of this sort might look to them and relations between them as the truth-makers for necessary truths. Red things are darker than pink things, and *necessarily* so. What makes this true? It is a relation between the property of being red and the property of being pink. And we can be acquainted not only with redness and pinkness but the relation of being darker than holding between redness and pinkness. Equilateral triangles are equiangular triangles, and *necessarily* so. What makes this true? It is a relation, one might argue, that holds between the property of being an equilateral triangle and the property of being an equiangular triangle, a relation with which one can be directly acquainted.

Nothing said here should convince you that there are universals (properties of a certain sort). The question of what makes two red things both red is a question that has occupied philosophers for literally thousands of years. Instead of universals, Plato famously talked about *forms*, and argued that with the right sort of intellectual training one can "see"[33] the nature of forms and bring before

---

[33] With the mind's "eye." How Plato understood talk of forms is a matter of considerable philosophical debate. Sometimes he seemed to think of the form of an X as a kind of ideal or model X – an ideal or model to which things can more or less approximate. Others would argue that Plato's talk of forms was just another way of talking about properties or universals.

the mind relations that hold between forms. Again, such a view might be hospitable to a foundationalism built on the idea of direct acquaintance.

There is a second view, however, about what grounds necessary truths. Some of the empiricists,[34] including, famously, David Hume, thought that some truths (what we would call necessary truths) depend on what he called relations between ideas (Hume 1888, 458). On this sort of view, the truth-maker for red being darker than pink would be a relation between the idea of redness and the idea of pinkness. Ideas and relations that hold between them are, again, the kind of things with which one can be directly acquainted. And somehow we are supposed to able to "read off" the nature of any possible reality that corresponds to ideas from what we know about those ideas and relations between them. The statement that triangles have three sides doesn't *seem* to be a description of ideas or relations between ideas. It seems to be a statement about triangles. But it also seems that one can discover the truth that triangles have three sides just by considering carefully the idea of a triangle and the idea of having three sides.

Again, one would need an entire (rather long) book to even attempt to make plausible any view about the truth-makers for necessary truths and the nature of our knowledge of such truths. It would be nice, however, if one could provide a unified account of foundational knowledge and I do think that the acquaintance theory has at least the potential to provide such an account.

2.3.1.1 Clarifications

The acquaintance theory sketched above distinguishes being in pain, being acquainted with pain, and the thought that one is in pain. It maintains that knowledge that one is in pain involves direct acquaintance with the pain while one is aware of the truth-making relation holding between the pain and one's thought that one is in pain. A creature might be capable of being in pain without being acquainted with that pain. And a creature might be capable of being acquainted with pain without having the thought that it is in pain, and, therefore, without having the capacity to be directly aware of the relevant "fit" between the thought and the pain.

Critics of direct acquaintance have sometimes raised as an objection to the view the fact that one might be acquainted with a very complex experience without knowing *that* the experience has the features with which one is acquainted. Suppose, for example, that one has a visual experience in

---

[34] It's not easy to define these philosophical terms of art. *Crudely*, empiricists thought that simple ideas are "copies" of prior sense experience, and that sense experience is the source of all knowledge and justified belief of the world. But this really is far too crude. Most empiricists thought that there were necessary truths and had various views about how we could know those truths.

which one's visual field contains something like thirty-six spots.[35] Surely that would *not* give most people a justified belief that, let alone *knowledge* that, one's visual experience has this feature. All of this seems right, but we have stressed that an acquaintance theorist insists that foundational justification or knowledge requires *more* than acquaintance with a feature of the world. It also requires thought and direct awareness of the correspondence between thought and that feature of the world that makes the thought true.[36] It is not quite clear what having the thought of thirty-six-spotted visual experience is, but it certainly seems doubtful that you or I could be aware of a truth-making relation between that feature of an experience and the relevant thought.

Neither is it even clear that one does have direct awareness of the relevant "thirty-six-spotted" character of the experience. Among the philosophers who think that there are properties or universals, many will distinguish among properties having different levels of determinacy or specificity. So think of the following properties we might describe a thing as having: being a bright cherry red, being cherry red, being dark red, being dark colored, being colored. It seems clear that we might describe a given thing correctly in any one of these different ways. And some philosophers are convinced that each of the above adjectives picks out a different property. They will concede, of course, that there are important dependency relations that exist among the properties. To use a term of art, the redness of this particular object x might supervene on (be determined by) its being cherry red, and being dark colored might supervene on its being red. Its being colored might supervene on all of more determine properties "below" (in terms of specificity) that property.

I'm certainly not arguing here that this metaphysical story of properties is correct, but if it is, one might acknowledge that when one is confronted with various properties along a continuum moving from greater specificity to more generality, one only notices (is directly acquainted with) *some* of the properties. And often, one might continue to argue, one is only directly acquainted with the more general property exemplified, not the highly specific property exemplified. That's why when the police question you as an eyewitness to a crime, you might be able to tell them accurately that you noticed a tall person get into a dark-colored car. When the police want more specific information – how tall, what specific color the car was – you might be unable to supply the

---

[35] A variation on what has come to be known as the problem of the speckled hen, originally discussed in Ushenko (1937). Ushenko, however, indicates that the example was originally suggested to him in conversation by H. H. Price).

[36] Thoughts are also "features" of the world. But thoughts can be true or false in virtue of the fact that they can correspond or fail to correspond to reality.

information. You noticed that the person was taller than average and you noticed that the car was dark-colored, but that's it.

That brings us back to the many-speckled visual field. Perhaps what one should say is that one is aware of the visual field's having the property of being "many-speckled" without being aware of its having the property of being "thirty-six-speckled". The former acquaintance might be part of what gives you noninferential knowledge of this general character of your experience; but in the absence of acquaintance with the more specific property, your foundations will not include the truth made true by the exemplification of *that* property. Of course, Raymond (that autistic savant in the movie *Rainman*) might be directly acquainted with much more of the intricate character of the world in which he finds himself, and his foundations might include far more in the way of specific truths about experience. Furthermore, you and I might *learn* to notice features of our experience of which we were previously unaware. We talked about the painter who learns to notice the many subtle changes in the character of visual experience due to changes in light and perspective. Studying the score of a symphony will often allow the student to notice the individual sounds of various instruments contributing to the overall blend of sounds of which we were previously aware.

Again, to settle precisely how best to respond to the plausible idea that the vast complexity of experience outstrips your ability to know various truths describing that experience, one needs to do some very difficult metaphysics and reach important conclusions about the nature of properties, thought, and the truth-making relation. One can't do epistemology in isolation, and we can't develop a plausible version of foundationalism without metaphysical insight.

Is the acquaintance theory a form of internalism? Well, we distinguished internal-state internalism from access internalism. We still haven't said much about what the objects of acquaintance *are*. We'll talk about this in the next section. For all I have said so far, one might be directly acquainted with features of the physical world. If one is, and one is acquainted with such features making true a thought about the physical world, then there will be foundational justification that is not a function (solely) of the internal states of a believer. In fact, most historically prominent proponents of the acquaintance theory argued that the objects of acquaintance are restricted to internal states and abstract objects. And if that view were true, that *would* lead one to embrace a form of internal-state internalism.

Does acceptance of the acquaintance theory commit one to *access* internalism? Not in any obvious way. One can certainly be acquainted with some state of the world X without even having the philosophical sophistication to *represent* such a relation as acquaintance. And without that conceptual sophistication one will not have any justified *beliefs* about the foundational justification provided by acquaintance. It may even be the case that one can be acquainted with something X without being acquainted with the fact that one is acquainted with X. Of course, there is a sense in which it might still be *possible* for someone who lacks philosophical concepts to acquire them. And it might be *possible* for someone to be acquainted with their acquaintance with X. But there is a limit to the complexity any finite being can hold before their mind.[37] In any event, it is not clear that acquaintance with one's acquaintance puts one in a better epistemic position with respect to the justification provided by the first-level justification.[38] And that's a good thing. The acquaintance theory wants to tie possession of noninferential justification to the satisfaction of philosophical curiosity. As I shall argue later, one hasn't hit on a plausible account of foundational justification and knowledge if one can possess that sort of justification and knowledge while still feeling that one needs to answer further questions in order to be in an intellectually satisfying state.

2.3.2 Other Forms of Internal-State Foundationalism

The acquaintance theory of foundational justification is only one internalist account of foundational justification. There are others. In the next section, I'll talk about Descartes's famous search for secure foundations on which to build all knowledge. But here, I'll briefly mention two other forms of internal-state internalism.

One is *epistemic conservatism*. According to the epistemic conservative, the mere fact that you find yourself believing something is at least some initial reason in support of what you believe. Even if what *you* believe seems to *us* completely crazy? Yes. But the epistemic conservative will be quick to point out that whatever initial reason you have for believing something might be outweighed by other factors. Given one way of thinking about epistemic conservatism, it is a view that bears at least a family resemblance to the coherence theory of justification discussed in Section 1. The coherence theorist is convinced that in seeking justification there is nowhere to look but one's beliefs. The epistemic conservative also thinks one doesn't *need* to escape one's beliefs to get at least some epistemic support for what one believes.

A close cousin to epistemic conservatism is *phenomenal* conservatism, a view most closely associated with Michael Huemer. Huemer (2001) distinguishes its *seeming* to one that P from one's believing that P. While not everyone is convinced that there is the relevant distinction, Huemer tries to convince you

---

[37] Who knows what an infinite, omniscient being might be able to know through acquaintance?
[38] More about this later.

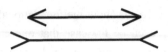

Figure 1 The Mueller-Lyer illusion

that there is by asking you think about something like the familiar Mueller-Lyer illusion (Figure 1).

Of the two straight line segments pictured in Figure 1, the first *seems* to be shorter than the second; Huemer will argue that this is true even when one is familiar with the illusion and isn't fooled into believing that the lines are of unequal length. In any event, Huemer argues that all epistemic justification bottoms out in what seems to you to be the case. Huemer will probably accept all of our earlier examples of plausible candidates for foundationally justified beliefs, but will argue that what gives us initial foundational justification for believing that we are in pain (when we are) or what justifies us in believing the axioms of Euclidean geometry, is that the respective claims just seem to us to be true. Like the epistemic conservative, the phenomenal conservative will be quick to point out that the initial justification a "seeming" gives us might be overridden by additional considerations (such as inconsistencies in what seems to us to be true).

Assuming that beliefs and "seemings" are internal states, both epistemic conservatism and phenomenal conservatism are forms of internal-state internalism.[39] Neither view is straightforwardly committed to *access* internalism. Arguably, one can believe something to be true without knowing that one believes it to be true or without even believing that one believes it to be true. Again, one might not have the conceptual sophistication to entertain thoughts about beliefs, even if one is perfectly able to form thoughts about experiences of various sorts. If one has the appropriate concepts, one might naturally believe that one believes P (when one believes P) and it might seem to one that it seems to one that P (when it does seem to one that P), but it is not clear that "second-order" beliefs and seemings add any weight to whatever epistemic force first-order beliefs and seemings are supposed to have.

---

[39] There is a serious complication I have been skirting. In addition to the internalism/externalism controversy in epistemology, there is an internalism/externalism controversy in the philosophy of mind. Really crudely, the controversy centers on what gives a belief or seeming (these along with states like desire or fear are called intentional states) the content it has. If intentional states represent the world as being a certain way, what makes it true that the state represents the world as being this way rather than another? The externalist thinks that it is the history of an intentional state that makes it the state that it is. Just as a photograph of you is a photograph of you because you figure in the causal explanation of how that image was created, so a thought of you is a thought of you because you figure (in the right sort of way) into a causal explanation of the thought. In what I say here, I'll be assuming that externalism about thought is not correct.

It is difficult to argue against epistemic or phenomenal conservatism. The pervasive worry is that both erect a kind of impenetrable "veil" of representations that "hides" from us the world as it really is. But that is probably just a way of making yet another plea for direct acquaintance as the satisfying way to end a regress of justification.

2.4 Externalist Foundationalism

In the limited space I have here, I'll sketch just two externalist accounts of foundational justification.[40] The worry about both is the same. I'll start by discussing a view suggested by David Armstrong (1973), and follow with a discussion of Alvin Goldman's (1979) reliabilism.

2.4.1 A Causal Account of Foundational Knowledge

Armstrong felt the pull of the idea that our knowledge of our own pain (and other sensations) doesn't require any sort of *inference*. But the most natural account of why this is so, he thought, is that we are just so constituted (or so designed)[41] that some of our states cause us (without the mediation of *other* beliefs) to believe that we are in such states. Some philosophers toyed with the idea of a more general "causal theory" of knowledge See Goldman (1967). The crude idea behind such a view is that we know that P when the fact that P (the fact that makes it true that P) causes (in the right sort of way)[42] our belief that P. But whether or not one is willing to embrace a view *that* general, one might find attractive the idea that *foundational* knowledge is nothing more than a direct (as in unmediated by other beliefs) causal connection between the fact that makes true what one believes and the fact that one has the belief.

I illustrated the idea of alleged foundational knowledge of this sort by using our old example of pain. But it is *conceivable*, of course, that *any* sort of fact might cause a belief in a way that doesn't involve the mediation of other beliefs. If certain forms of theism are true, perhaps there is a God who just inspires people to believe in His existence (where the divine intervention does not require the believer to rely on any sort of inference). And if the world were like this, belief in the existence of God might be foundationally justified/known.

---

[40] There is another volume in this series that discusses the internalism/externalism controversy.

[41] Plantinga (1993) suggests that we understand epistemically rational belief (he preferred "warranted" beliefs) in terms of beliefs formed in the way in which we are "designed" to form beliefs (at least when we are in the "right" sort of environment). Plantinga himself understood design in terms of a creator design plan, but invites his readers to come up with an alternative (if they can).

[42] The proponent of this view will always need this qualification to avoid objections that conjure up really "weird" causal chains that even the causal theorist won't want to generate knowledge.

For some of us that is worrisome. The concern is not that theism is implausible. It is, rather, that the existence of a God isn't the *kind* of thing that one can know directly (without inference).[43] I'll say more about this concern later.

2.4.2 Reliabilism

The causal theorist described above understands foundationally justified belief/knowledge in terms of the causal origin of a belief – the *history* of a belief. The reliabilist has a similar view. Goldman (1979) quite explicitly adopts a recursive analysis of justification. He *is* a foundationalist (although he will be quick to point out his foundationalism is quite different from *traditional* foundationalism). The "base clause" on which he relies in recursively analyzing justification is the idea of what he called a belief-independent, unconditionally *reliable* belief-producing process. Think of beliefs as the "output" of causal processes that take as "input" all sorts of different stimuli (including sometimes other beliefs). When the input to a process *does* include beliefs, those beliefs would need to be *justified* in order for the process to generate other justified beliefs (remember the slogan: garbage in, garbage out). The process producing the belief would also need to be *conditionally* reliable – the process must result in mostly true beliefs *when* the input beliefs are true. But belief-*independent* processes take as their inputs something other than beliefs, and their reliability consists in the fact that most beliefs generated by this sort of process are true (the process is unconditionally reliable).[44] One's pain, for example, might typically cause one to believe that one is in pain. How is this different from the causal theory discussed in the previous section? The belief-independent processes that yield mostly true beliefs need not *always* yield true beliefs. So, for the reliabilist, there might be a cause of my belief that I had a pain earlier today, and the cause of that belief might *not* be the fact that I was in pain. Still, whatever process resulted in the belief might be such that it *usually* produces true beliefs.

Like the causal theory, reliabilism implies that it is at least *conceivable* that *any* sort of belief might be foundationally justified. On the view whether we are foundationally justified in believing P is an empirical question that depends on whether the belief is produced by a belief-independent, unconditionally reliable

---

[43] Again, this isn't the place to get a sympathetic evaluation of externalist accounts of knowledge and justification.

[44] We are *sketching* an account. There are all kinds of complex "in-house" controversies among reliabilists about how to understand reliability. (See Connee and Felmdan 1998). And there is a technical problem that introspective knowledge of what one believes might take as its input a belief, even though one wouldn't think of the output (a belief about that belief) as involving inference See Wilson (2003).

process. We can imagine reliable belief-independent processes that produce beliefs that there is a God, that there is an afterlife, that *Crazy Legs* will win the eighth race at Belmont.[45]

The reliabilist rejects access requirement on justification, so one might have a reliably produced, foundationally justified belief even if one has no idea *how* the belief was produced, or indeed, *that* it was produced in a reliable way. And more traditional foundationalists will find it counterintuitive that justified belief can be severed in this way from the kind of justification traditional epistemologists sought – a kind of justification that would bring with it *assurance* of truth.

Although the following argument is a bit crude, consider this. Suppose you are trying to figure out what you know or, at least, what you are justified in believing. And suppose I tell you that it really isn't all that complicated, at least with respect to foundational knowledge and justified belief. You directly know that P when you believe P without inference and P is true. And you are noninferentially justified in believing P when you believe P without inference and P is true. Given this view, you *might* have all sorts of foundational knowledge and justified belief. But merely having true belief wasn't what you were after, right? You already knew that your beliefs might be true and that they might be false. You wanted to *know*, or at least have *justification*, for thinking that your beliefs are true? "Knowledge" or "justified belief" that doesn't bring with it any assurance of truth isn't worth having. It doesn't satisfy intellectual curiosity. Or so argue the critics of externalism.

The need to tie epistemic justification to the satisfaction of epistemic curiosity has always been the concern of traditional philosophers who sought a secure foundation on which to build safely the rest of what we believe. In the next section, we turn to the search for assurance.

3 What Belongs in the Foundations?

We have sketched some quite different accounts of foundational justification and knowledge, and I have indicated my sympathy for a very traditional sort of foundationalism that invokes the idea of direct acquaintance with various aspects of reality, including facts about the correspondence that holds between true thoughts and the facts that make those thoughts true. Outside of giving some initially plausible examples of truths that might satisfy our requirements for noninferentially justified belief or direct knowledge, we haven't said much

---

[45] There is a great short story by D. H. Lawrence, *The Rocking Horse Winner*, which tells the story of a boy who reliably forms beliefs about the outcome of horse races by maniacally riding his rocking horse.

about how to *decide* what belongs in the foundations on which we must build the rest of what we justifiably believe.

3.1 Descartes's Search for Secure Foundationalism

Descartes may be the philosopher most famously associated with the view that ideal knowledge must be built on secure foundations. A discussion of his view has, so far, been conspicuous by its absence. I am going to talk about it here, but primarily to link his search for secure foundations to the acquaintance theorist's criteria for determining when we have acquaintance that yields noninferential justification and knowledge.

Descartes (1960) began his search for secure foundations by reminding us of how much disagreement there is among even very learned people. He seemed to suggest that this should lead us to be concerned that we might be accepting dogmatically hypotheses just because they seem initially obvious or just because we have been told by others that they are true. To find *secure* foundations on which to build an edifice of knowledge, he suggested that we employ what has been called the method of doubt. The basic idea is that we reject as an inappropriate *foundation* on which to build something that we believe when we can even *imagine* a way in which we could have what we take to be our justification while what we believe is false. Rather than consider our beliefs one by one, he suggested that we proceed by thinking about *kinds* of belief. Let's see what we are left with if we follow Descartes's advice.

I believe that I was born in Toronto. Without worrying too much about what justification I have for that belief, is the justification available to me consistent with my belief's being false? Of course, it is. My parents might have been fugitives on the run who invented a false history for my sisters and me to help throw investigators off the scent. Generalizing, it wouldn't be hard for Cartesians to convince themselves that there is the *possibility* of error whenever we rely on the *testimony* of others (oral or written). And just think of how many of our beliefs rely on such testimony.

Let's cut to the chase though. Everything we believe about a physical world that exists independently of us requires relying on the "testimony" of the five senses. If beliefs about the physical world based on vivid sense experience don't survive the method of doubt, we will have foreclosed inclusion in the foundations an *enormous* number of beliefs. Descartes seemed to argue (at least *initially*) that we can *conceive* of error even here.[46] It is at least *possible* to have a dream that you can't distinguish from veridical experience. It is at least

---

[46] Descartes is so famously associated with his arguments for skepticism that we sometimes fail to mention that he eventually renounced his skeptical worries as foolish.

possible that some malevolent being has the power to induce in you massive hallucinatory experience that leads you to all sorts of false conclusions about the world around you.[47] If foundational justification precludes the possibility of error, we will need to retreat to truths about our internal mental life to find that sort of justification. If that internal life includes awareness of the truth-makers for necessary truths, then we might also retain foundational justification for *that* sort of belief.

When he was engaged in what is sometimes called "hyperbolic" doubt, Descartes seemed to suggest that we are *fallible* even with respect to elementary logical and arithmetic truths. That demon capable of inducing hallucinations might even cause you to believe that $2 + 2 = 5$.[48] That admission was potentially fatal to Descartes's ultimate attempt to recover what we ordinarily take ourselves to know. Any argument (including some rather complicated arguments that Descartes employed) will rely on our ability to know at least logical principles. But my main reason for bringing up Descartes at all is to tie *his* approach to finding secure foundations to the acquaintance theorist's reasons for adopting a similarly restrictive view as to what should be included in foundational justification/knowledge.

3.2 Fallible Justification and Foundational Justification

The acquaintance theorist seeks to end a regress of justification by locating a kind of justification based (in part) on direct awareness of truth-makers. But how do we figure out with what we are directly acquainted? As we discussed, acquaintance is a *relation* we have to the truth-maker for a belief. But why not suppose that in perception, for example, we are directly acquainted with facts about the physical world? Why not assume that when we see a red, round object we are directly acquainted with the fact that something physical is red and round? For that matter, why shouldn't we assume that we are directly acquainted with the fact of God's existence?

At this point, the acquaintance theorist will engage in thought experiments that should remind us of Descartes's search for secure foundations. You believe that there is before you, right now, a tomato. Are you directly acquainted with the existence of a tomato? Well, imagine that instead of seeing a tomato, you are seeing a very realistic wax imitation of a tomato.[49] Assuming that you have no reason to suspect that the tomato isn't real, wouldn't you still have the same

---

[47] This is the grist for the mill of much science fiction. The Martians in Bradbury's *The Martian Chronicles* had this ability. So did the creatures who figured in the pilot episode of *Start Trek*. And so did the computers that figured so prominently in *The Matrix*.

[48] Think of the villain in *1984* who (through torture) convinced Winston that $2 + 2 = 5$.

[49] The example is from H. H. Price (1932).

justification for believing that there is a tomato there even when there isn't? If the answer is "Yes," then the justification you have in the "good" case (the case where there is a tomato there) can't be direct acquaintance with the fact that there is a tomato there. You certainly aren't acquainted with a tomato's existence in the "bad" case (the case where it is a wax imitation).

But let's retreat to the more modest claim that there is *some* physical object that is red and roundish before you. Aren't you acquainted with *that* fact? Remember Descartes's warning. Couldn't you have the *same* justification for believing that there is a physical object there that is red and round even if you are having a vivid dream (or drug-induced, demon-induced, computer-induced) hallucination. Again, call these nonveridical experiences "bad" cases. In the bad cases, you aren't directly acquainted with something physical's being red and round – there is no *physical* object that is red and round with which you can be acquainted. If the justification you have in the bad case is the *same* as the justification you have in the good case, then it isn't direct acquaintance with a physical object that is red and round in the good case either.

If this sort of argument should convince us that we don't have direct awareness of the relevant truth-makers in these cases, similar arguments are obviously available in a host of other cases. You believe that you had eggs for breakfast (or at least experiences *as of* having eggs). Why? Because you seem to remember having had the relevant experiences. Can you have this sort of justification even though what you believe is false? At my age, you don't need much of an argument to convince yourself that the answer is "Yes." But if it is, then your justification in the "good" case (the case where memory *is* veridical) can't be direct awareness of a past state of the world. After all, we have conceded that whatever justification you have in the good case would be available in the bad case, and when memory plays you false, you certainly aren't directly aware of something that *didn't* happen.

Our method for finding foundational knowledge/justification will also rule out for inclusion in our foundations beliefs about the mental states of others (the problem of other minds). I do think that there are other people, not just other bodies. I believe that I am not the only person who thinks, feels, and senses. But it seems almost obvious to some of us that all I have to rely on in reaching conclusions about others is physical behavior[50] – behavior that can mislead me with respect to what's going on in a mind. It's not even that hard to fake pain, sympathy, happiness, and sorrow. Good actors can get you to form all sorts of

---

[50] This is tricky. In describing physical movement as behavior, I am probably already presupposing that the movement is guided by mind. It might be best, then, to translate all the talk about behavior here into talk of physical movement of physical things. I'll continue, however, to talk of behavior.

false belief about their "inner" mental life. If the justification you have in the "good" cases (the cases where what you believe is true) is the same as the justification you have in the "bad" cases (the cases where you have been duped) then in neither case are you directly aware of the mental life of another person.

The pattern of argument sketched above resembles closely the Cartesian method of doubt. And that's because when we have fallible justification, we'll be able to think of a situation that from the subject's perspective[51] is indistinguishable from the case in which our putative justification leads to true belief, but in which the belief is instead false. And, trivially, when your belief is false, you can't be directly acquainted with the truth-maker for that belief.

3.3 A "Disjunctivist" Response

A key premise of the above arguments is that the available justification is the *same* in the "good" and the "bad" cases. Whether I am veridically perceiving objects in my immediate environment or I am suffering a vivid hallucination, my beliefs about the objects I take to be there are equally justified. Whether I actually remember or just seem to remember putting my glasses on the bookshelf, I have the same sort of justification for believing what I do about the past.

The disjunctivist rejects this step in the argument. In general, just because we don't notice (or are even *unable* to notice) a distinction between X and Y it doesn't follow that X and Y aren't different. This is obviously the case when the difference between X and Y involves relational properties. I probably don't have the skill to distinguish a really good forgery of a Renoir painting from the real thing. But we wouldn't want to infer from this that a forgery of this sort couldn't exist. Even when we restrict ourselves to the "intrinsic" character of the two paintings, we still shouldn't conclude that there *couldn't* be differences between the paintings that are undetectable by people like *me*.

Experiences aren't paintings. But perhaps one should be justifiably wary of concluding that two experiences are of the same sort just because we can't tell the difference (from our subjective introspective perspective) between the two. Again, we are not talking about relational properties of experiences. It is probably true *by definition* that hallucinatory experiences have different causes from the experiences that are, in fact, veridical. But even when we restrict ourselves to the intrinsic character of experiences, why should we assume that two experiences have the same intrinsic character just because we don't notice any differences between them?

---

[51] This is the expression Bergmann (2006) uses in one of the best critiques of the kind of foundationalism I defend.

Williamson (2000) underscores the concern by asking you to consider very gradual changes over time in the character of a sensation. At time $t + 1$ I feel cold and at $t + 1000$ I feel warm and at every moment between $t + 1$ and $t + 1000$ there is a very subtle change along the continuum. Don't you find it plausible to assume that there is some point along the continuum where you won't know whether you feel cold or not, and doesn't that suggest that we don't always have unproblematic epistemic access to the character of this kind of sensation?

I have argued elsewhere (Fumerton 2016) that there are borderline cases and that even when we are directly aware of the determinate (the very specific) character of an experience, we might not have awareness of *paradigmatic* correspondence between a thought that the experience is of a certain *general* sort and that *determinate* fact. In some cases, we might not even have a thought that represents the experience other than the *demonstrative* thought – the thought that the experience is *that* kind of experience. In borderline cases, we might have a *weak* sort of justification provided by the relevant acts of direct awareness. But we need to move slowly before we draw more extravagant metaphysical or epistemological conclusions about our access to our inner mental states.

The Cartesian argument for the conclusion that we are never directly acquainted with physical objects in visual experience compares *veridical* experience (the kind of experience you have when you actually see the object) with *nonveridical* experience (like a vivid hallucination). The argument is that we should treat the justification as the same in both cases. Some disjunctivists will insist that in the right sort of perception we are directly aware of at least some facts about the physical world. In hallucinatory experiences, they concede, we are not. These disjunctivists often don't offer much of an account of what we *are* aware of in hallucination other than to say that it is a state that we confuse with direct awareness of aspects of physical reality.

Disjunctivists are presumably going to be forced into the uncomfortable position of offering two *radically* different accounts of what is going on in veridical and vivid, nonveridical experience. And we seem to be lacking any sort of plausible *explanation* of why we can't tell the two apart. The traditional foundationalist offers an explanation. In both veridical and nonveridical experience there is an experiential "common denominator." Both involve a sensation that is (we think) *caused* in different ways. The view fits rather nicely with what we *believe* (justifiably or not) about the *immediate* causes of sensation. The familiar visual experience that we associate with seeing a table has as its *direct* cause (we think) a brain state. Light reflects off the surface of an object (no sensation yet), changes occur in the retina (no sensation yet), the signal is carried to a certain region of the brain, and, finally, the sensation occurs.

Dreams and hallucinations can occur because the relevant neural events can occur as a result of a variety of more remote causes. Again, this is the story we are told about how experiences occur. And the story seems to suggest that our access to the physical world is only through the sensation that is (we think) the end product of certain causal chains. It is the *sensation* with which we are directly acquainted.

There are many different accounts of how to understand sensations. Some argue that sensations just are brain states. Others think that sensations are the direct effects of brain states but are in some important sense not physical. In this camp, there are still all sorts of dispute about exactly how to understand the metaphysics of sensation. Some *sense-datum* theorists argue that even in hallucinatory experience we are aware of *objects* having various properties (sense datum) – it's just that the objects are not *physical* objects in *physical* space. Adverbial theorists think that it is best to construe different sensations as different *ways* of sensing, where these ways of sensing involve no object (other than perhaps the self that in is is in the relevant state).[52] The acquaintance theory is compatible with all sorts of different accounts of sensations provided that sensations remain something of which one can be directly acquainted and represented in thought.[53]

3.4 Meager Foundations on which to Build?

The concern with anything like Cartesian criteria for finding secure foundations is that the price for such security is a foundation too insubstantial on which to build. This worry no doubt accounts for the attraction externalism holds for many foundationalists. Depending on how cooperative the world is, reliabilism, for example, might allow for foundational justification and knowledge concerning some aspects of the past, the physical world, other minds, and even the future.

In prefacing his discussion of skepticism with regard to the senses, Hume (1888, Part I, Sec. II) poetically warned that those seeking rational assurance for what they believe should realize that:

> Nature has not left this to his choice, and has doubtless, esteemed it an affair of too great importance to be trusted to our uncertain reasonings and speculations.

---

[52] It's called the adverbial theory because its proponents think that one should think of expressions like "pain" in the sentence "I feel pain" as functioning as a kind of "disguised" adverb modifying the way of feeling. Some will invent "ugly" adverbs like "red-ly" and "round-ly" to describe the way of appearing that is associated with seeing or hallucinating something red and round.

[53] There are even acquaintance theorists who toy with the idea of supposing that when *introspecting* one can be directly aware of at least some features of the brain. Russell (1948) *might* have suggested such a view.

Although some externalists might use this passage to argue that Hume was a proto-externalist, it seems much more likely to me that Hume was one of those interested in seeking a *rational* basis for beliefs that *may* have causes unrelated to the possession of epistemic justification. Indeed, Hume seemed to me to support *unequivocally* a rather extreme skeptical position with respect to justified belief about the external world (and for that matter about the future).[54] In the passage quoted above, Hume was obviously willing to admit that we might have reliably produced beliefs about the physical world, and even that it wouldn't be at all surprising to him if there were many reliably produced beliefs that didn't result from inference. But I don't think that he would be at all sympathetic to the suggestion that the existence of such reliably produced beliefs would do anything for the philosopher seeking a rational basis for belief. He wanted his intellectual curiosity satisfied, and he realized that satisfying externalist conditions for foundational knowledge or justified belief just wouldn't accomplish that goal.

Externalists will often be quick to point out that skepticism is the inevitable result of a philosophy that restricts the foundations for knowledge and justified belief to beliefs accompanied by direct acquaintance with truth-makers.[55] It is bad enough that we might excise from our foundations all beliefs about the external world. But it is also hard to see how we can be directly acquainted with *past* states of the world. Vivid apparent memory doesn't seem to be direct awareness. That's precisely why we don't have any difficulty understanding how a belief based on even vivid apparent memory might nevertheless be false.

With what are we left? It looks as if our foundations consist of truths describing the *present* contents of our mind and truths describing whatever abstract entities (like properties) with which we are *presently* acquainted. To be sure, some philosophers (James 1890; Broad 1923, 1938) have tried to expand slightly that *present*. These philosophers talked about a *specious* present, a "thick" expanse of time that it is the object of an equally "thick" relation of direct acquaintance. Others, like Mill (1963–91, vol. 7) and an earlier Russell (1959) seemed to just "give" themselves knowledge of past experience. Mill specifically tries to preempt possible criticism with a kind of impatient shrug of the shoulders pointing out that everyone is going to rely on memory – where are we going without it? Do we need to choose between

---

[54] He was strangely silent about the possibility of rational belief about the past.

[55] Although they might well reject even the intelligibility of direct acquaintance.

secure foundations and a skepticism with respect to the rest of what we believe?

4 Traditional Foundationalism and the Challenge of Skepticism

We ended the last section worried that our search for secure foundations on which to build might leave us in a position where we must try to erect the huge edifice of our commonsense beliefs on a foundation too small to support the weight of that edifice. We'll begin this section by considering whether we should let a commitment to avoiding skepticism dictate the nature of our foundationalism. We'll then look at the tools available to the philosopher trying to build on foundations. More specifically, we'll ask what principles of inference might be plausibly *included* in the foundations of knowledge and justified belief.

4.1 Should We Reject Skepticism from the Start?

Chisholm (1966) famously suggested that the epistemologist should commit at the outset to making whatever moves are necessary to avoid skepticism. While the interpretation of Moore (1959) is a bit more complicated, he, too, seemed to suggest that when a philosophical theory leads to skepticism, that's a reason to conclude that something is wrong with that theory.[56] Do Chisholm and Moore have the right approach?

Later in this section, we'll explore the ways in which traditional foundationalists might try to escape skepticism. But we should begin by reflecting on the question of whether philosophers should reject at the outset any view that leads to skepticism. Before we do, however, we should very briefly consider different forms of skepticism.

One can be a skeptic about the possibility of *knowledge* or a skeptic about the possibility of *justified belief*. One can also be a *global* skeptic (a skeptic with respect to the possibility of *every* sort of knowledge or justified belief) or a *local* skeptic (a skeptic with respect only to certain *kinds* of knowledge or justified belief). The global knowledge skeptic asserts that we don't know anything at all. That view seems to entail that we don't even know that we don't know anything. The global skeptic with respect to justified belief asserts even more dramatically

---

[56] Even if you can't figure out precisely *what* is wrong with that theory. Ironically, perhaps, Moore was a very traditional sort of foundationalist who understood full well the difficulty of recovering "commonsense" from the foundations to which he was committed. Chisholm, in particular, might have been heavily influenced by Reid (1764) who emphasized his commitment to an epistemology that is guided by "commonsense" and made clear that he found simply absurd the posturing of philosophical skeptics.

that we have no justified beliefs. And that view seems to entail that we aren't even justified in believing that we don't have any justified beliefs.

Some philosophers think that it is a kind of "rule" of communication that one shouldn't make an assertion one doesn't know to be true.[57] Others think that, at the very least, one shouldn't make an assertion if one has no reason to believe it to be true. If knowledge is the "norm" of assertion in the above sense, then the global knowledge skeptic seems to be *trying* to violate the rule. If justified belief is the norm of assertion, then the global skeptic about justified belief seems to be *trying* to violate that rule. I suspect, however, that most skeptics would not be particularly bothered by the fact that their assertions might not respect these sorts of "rule." Philosophers, more generally, seem to be often interested in making assertions primarily to start debate and discussion. To create a problem, you don't need to know how to fix it.

In any event, it is very difficult to find global skeptics either about knowledge or justified belief. Hume is one of the most interesting and influential philosophers who seemed to embrace a number of skeptical theses. He argued for the view that we have no justification for believing anything about a perceiver-independent world, and no justification for believing any contingent proposition describing the future. But he thought we did know that we have certain perceptions.[58] And he thought we could know truths that depend on "relations between ideas."

Is the thesis that we can't have knowledge or justified beliefs about the physical world an absurd thesis? Isn't it just obvious that we can trust experiences as a reliable indicator of what the world that causes those experiences is like? In thinking about this question it is useful to remind ourselves that philosophers worried a great deal about perception in the seventeenth and eighteenth centuries as science developed more and more sophisticated ways of magnifying the reality that we take to be causally responsible for sense experience. Under that magnification, the world of "common sense" starts to disappear.[59] Flat, solid, colored, motionless surfaces of objects became spatially separated, colorless objects moving at incredible speeds. And according to

---

[57] Most famously Williamson (2000). Williamson would allow that one might violate the rule and still be blameless. If you haven't received a very good education, you might frequently violate rules of grammar, and we might not think that you are at fault. Some grammatical rules are probably violated by most people most of the time, but that doesn't stop them from being the rules of grammar.

[58] This is tricky. There are famous passages in which Hume seems to deny that there is a self. If he does, it will be difficult for Hume to identify the subject that is aware of perceptions. But Hume also cryptically abandons his skepticism about the existence of a self, and it might be precisely because he saw the seriousness of this problem (Hume 1888, Appendix 635).

[59] Eddington (1929) famously discussed the puzzles caused by scientific advances when he talks about "two" tables – the smooth-surfaced, solid table ordinary people have beliefs about and

some contemporary theoretical physicists, even those objects themselves threaten to disappear in favor of "fields" of one sort or another. There is a *philosophical* problem of how to justify reliance on appearance to reach conclusions about a perceiver-independent reality. But there is also a problem created by science *itself* concerning which appearances are the best indicators of what the world is really like. One could make the argument that science has left "commonsense" behind long ago.

It is partly in light of the above considerations that Russell (1940) famously suggested that commonsense leads to science and science leads to the rejection of commonsense. To evaluate fully this idea, one would need to carefully reflect on just what the contents of ordinary beliefs about the physical world are. I have argued (Fumerton 2002) that everyday beliefs are actually neutral on the *intrinsic* character of the physical world. But the defense of that view is long and complicated.

Just as scientific investigation can lead one to worry about how precisely perceptual appearance reflects reality, so also science itself suggests that we should be more worried than we usually are about relying on apparent memory to reach conclusions about the past. Many who do research in this field suggest that at best memory doesn't deliver much accurate *detail* about many past experiences.[60] Rather it delivers a kind of "pointillist" sketch of the past, a sketch that we fill in with our imagination. Hard-core skeptics are going to worry about how one could justify this sort of position without already begging the question by relying on memory, but it is at least provocative that even after one thinks that one has found a way to escape more extreme skepticism, science might lead us to reexamine our reliance on various "unproblematic" sources of information that science presupposes.

4.2 Inferential Justification and Principles of Reasoning

When we discussed the epistemic regress argument for foundationalism, we noted that there may be not just one, but infinitely many, potential regresses that we need to stop in order to allow for the possibility of justified beliefs. That's because at least some epistemologists accept the view that I have called elsewhere (Fumerton 1996) *inferential internalism*. That's the view that for one to be justified in believing P on the basis of E one needs not only justification for believing that E, but also justification for believing that E makes

---

think about, and the table that consists of tiny particles spatially removed from one another moving at incredible speeds.

[60] A great deal depends on how such a thesis gets fleshed out. There are important differences among apparent memories of what just happened, apparent memories of what happened a couple of hours ago, and apparent memories about what happened years, or even decades, ago.

probable P.[61] If the only way to justify our belief is to *infer* what is believed from something else, then we would need to infer that E makes probable P from something else F. And we would need to infer that F makes probable that E makes probable that P from something else G, and so on, ad infinitum. If we accept inferential internalism, then to get beyond our foundations employing nondeductive reasoning, we will need to get direct access to the truth of at least some epistemic principles made true by relations of making probable holding between propositions.

Access externalists allow for justified beliefs even if the person with that justified belief has no access to the fact that they *are* justified. Inferential *externalists*, may require that inferential justification involves *legitimate* reasoning, but they will not require for inferential justification that we have *access* to what rules of inferences we follow or access to the fact that the rules in question are legitimate. (If you wonder how one can "follow" a rule without knowing what the rule is, think about most people who follow *very* complex rules of grammar when speaking, but who almost certainly couldn't identify the complex rules of grammar that they follow).

Earlier I warned against accepting general access requirements on justification. But requiring access to the legitimacy of the *reasoning* one employs is a different matter. Suppose I infer some very complex theorem in mathematics M from premises E, and suppose, further, that the fact that I get a tingling feeling in my spine when I think about M being true when I believe that E is what causes me to believe M. Further, suppose that E does entail M but that the entailment is far too difficult for *me* to grasp. Would we really want to allow that I am justified in believing M? Probably not, right? But what is missing? One obvious suggestion is that I haven't *grasped* the relevant connection between E and M. The relevant grasping could be understood as knowledge or justified belief that the relevant connection obtains. But I have also argued elsewhere (Fumerton 2018) that one might understand the grasping as a kind of awareness that falls short of belief.

So again, if the *inferential internalists* are right, then to build on foundations, we will need access to principles that allow the relevant inferences. To end regress, we will need *direct* access to at least some such principles. What are the best candidates? We'll obviously want to sanction the principles of deductive logic that license deductively valid inferences. We can just "see"[62] that 1) the proposition that if P then Q, together with 2) the proposition that P, *entails* (guarantees the truth of) 3) the proposition that Q. We can just "see" that the

---

[61] Where entailment is the upper limit of making probable. See Huemer (2002) and Carroll (1895) for objections to the view.

[62] I put the "see" in scare quotes to underscore that it is an intellectual insight – not a visual experience of some sort.

proposition 1) if P then Q together with the proposition 2) not-Q entails the truth of 3) the proposition that not-P, and so on for the various principles the legitimacy of which one studies in a course on formal logic.[63]

Unfortunately, deduction won't take one very far. If our premises really are ultimately restricted to descriptions of the current contents of our minds and descriptions of abstract entities (like properties and relations between properties), it's hard to see how deduction will get us to the physical world, the past, the future, and other minds (let alone the more exotic entities postulated by theoretical physics). Perhaps, however, we also have direct access to principles that tell us that there are relations *of making probable* that hold between propositions.

One candidate for a principle of this sort is a principle that sanctions induction (also called enumerative induction).[64] By observing a great many Fs that have been G (without ever observing an F that hasn't been a G, we might infer that the next F we find will be G, or even that all (or most) Fs are G. Russell (1959) suggested that these sorts of inference might be sanctioned by the following principles:

a) The greater the number of cases in a which a thing of the sort A has been found associated with a thing of the sort B, the more probable it is (if no cases of failure of association are known) that A is always associated with B.

b) Under the same circumstances, a sufficient number of cases of the association of A with B will make it nearly certain that A is always associated with B, and will make this general law approach certainty without limit.

Although he didn't put it quite this way, it is clear that Russell suggested that a) and b) should be considered necessary truths that can be known without inference.[65]

Even if Russell convinces you of this, inductive reasoning, like deductively valid reasoning, seems to have severe limitations. It hard to see how one could use induction to infer the existence of one *kind* of thing from an entirely *different* sort of thing. And it is important to note that induction won't be of any use in the fight against skepticism unless one can solve the problem of memory and move

---

[63] More carefully, perhaps we should just suggest that most people are capable of "seeing" the entailment in *particular* cases. Arguably, developing a logic requires *generalization* of a sort that involves much more sophistication. And some entailments might be very difficult to "see." The "Monty Hall" puzzle might convince you of this. The problem is highlighted by Marilyn vos Savant (1990). There are many other logical puzzles like this that are very difficult to solve even though most of us are *capable* of finding the solution.

[64] There isn't terminological conformity. Some philosophers use the expression "inductive reasoning" to refer to any sort of reasoning that isn't deductively valid. Others use the expression more narrowly (as I do here).

[65] I think that he eventually changed his mind about this – see Russell (1948).

from premises describing what one seems to remember to conclusions about what has actually happened. The premises of inductive arguments describe *past* associations.

Consider the first problem. How could we ever establish subjective appearance as a reliable indicator of objective reality? We certainly don't seem to be able to establish through past experience a *correlation* between appearances, on the one hand, and appearance-independent reality, on the other. After all, we can't step out from "behind" appearance to get a "peek" at a world that exists independently of our experiences. We can correlate one sort of sensation with another sort of sensation, but how do we correlate sensation with something other than a sensation?[66]

Some have argued that positing a physical world is just obviously the best *explanation* for our subjective sensations coming and going the way they do. To help with our current problem, we would need to take a claim about one explanation beating out competitors to be the kind of claim that can be known or justifiably believed *without inference*.[67] And that's a tall order. At the very least it seems that often our reason for thinking that a given explanation is plausible is that it resembles others that have turned out to be correct – a kind of inductive argument for the plausibility of the explanation.[68]

In some ways, the problem of justifying one's reliance on apparent memory is an even more fundamental epistemological problem. It certainly doesn't seem that one can *inductively* establish the reliability of memory. After all, as noted above, induction reaches conclusions relying on *past* correlations of kinds of thing. Eventually, one would presumably need to rely on memory to acquire the relevant premises of an inductive argument for the reliability of memory. One could, of course, argue that one's seeming to remember having had a given experience E just does make (at least initially) likely that one had the

---

[66] Some philosophers like Berkeley and Hume seemed to reach an even stronger conclusion – the conclusion that we can't even *think* of a world that is independent of appearance. Hume puts his conclusion this way:

> Let us chace our imaginations to the heavens, or to the utmost limits of the universe; we never really advance a step beyond ourselves, nor can conceive of any kind of existence, but those perceptions which have appear'd in that narrow compass. This is the universe of the imagination, nor have we have any idea but what is there produc'd.
>
> (1988, pp. 67–8)

[67] More carefully, we would need to be able to know a) that the appearances in question have an explanation, and b) that the physical world hypothesis is more likely to be true than the disjunction of all other possible explanations (a disjunction is just a complex statement that combines statements into a complex statement using the word "or.")

[68] Again, science might actually seem to throw a wrench in the works by positing radical indeterminism at the microlevel. On one interpretation, the idea is that somethings happen without having a *causal* explanation.

experience. And one could further suggest that we should include *this* principle in the foundations of knowledge and justified belief.

The above suggests a "recipe" for responding to the charge that traditional foundationalism leads to skepticism. One can "give" oneself foundational knowledge or justified belief in as many principles of reasoning as one needs in order to avoid skepticism.[69] As we discussed earlier, a real shortcut is a close cousin of epistemic conservatism. Someone sympathetic to epistemic conservatism might argue that the assertion that believing P makes (initially) likely that P is a *necessary* truth that should be included in the foundations of knowledge and justified belief. Huemer (2001) would presumably argue that one can include in one's foundations the principle that its seeming to one that P makes (initially) likely that P.[70]

Is the traditional foundationalist "home free" in avoiding a skepticism that might initially seem to follow from the restricted foundations with which they have to work? Perhaps *dialectically*. But one wants to make epistemological moves with a clear conscience. You need to convince yourself that you can find an interpretation of "making probable" that allows you to *plausibly* conclude that you are directly aware of the truth-makers for epistemic principles that describe one proposition as making probable another.[71]

I have earlier expressed reservations about supposing that one can foundationally know (or justifiably believe) that a given explanation is the best explanation available for some observed phenomenon. Inductive reasoning, by contrast, seems to be a much more plausible candidate for a principle that has that place in the hierarchy of knowledge. Perhaps, there is even some hope for the idea that it is a *necessary* truth that when most observed Fs have been G then it is *likely* that most Fs are Gs.[72]

If we do have direct access to the legitimacy of inductive reasoning, and we do have access to a specious present (a thick chunk of the passage of experience), it may not be completely implausible to try an inductive justification of the reliability of apparent memory.[73] As we noted earlier, we are bombarded at every moment of our conscious life with an array of experiences. And, at each moment in time, we seem to remember, or are at least capable of seeming to

---

[69] It seems to me that this is, essentially, the approach that Chisholm (1966) took to defeating skepticism.

[70] Although he *wouldn't* think that you need to know this truth *in order for* your "seemings" to get you the relevant justification.

[71] The basic idea behind the view that one can find such a relation of making probable was advanced by the famous economist (but also influential philosopher) John Maynard Keynes (1921).

[72] It is obviously *not* a necessary truth that if most *observed* Fs have been G then most Fs are G.

[73] I choose my words carefully. An inductive argument for the reliability of memory will strike many as tilting at windmills.

remember, a host of experiences we had a moment earlier. If we can hold *both* the apparent memories, and the experiences that they are memories of, before our mind we can generate quickly (and repeatedly) inductive justification for the reliability of apparent memory.

There are other epistemic principles that we haven't discussed yet but that might also be of use in battling the skeptic. One is the so-called principle of indifference. If you have no more reason to believe P than not-P, then it would be irrational to think that P is more likely to be true than not-P. If there are seven mutually exclusive alternatives, P, Q, R, S, T, U, and V, and there is no reason to think that any one is more likely to be true than any of the others, then it seems that one should think that each of the alternatives is *unlikely* to be true, *and* that not-P is more likely than P, that not-Q is more likely than Q, and so on. That's because in the absence of any relevant evidence, the hypotheses are all equally likely to be true.

When attempting to apply the principle of indifference one must be careful to "partition" the possibilities properly. When one has no idea at all what color shirt someone just bought it would be an almost obvious mistake to reason that since it is either red or not-red and I have no information that bears on the color, the probability of its being red is 50 percent. Crudely, the problem with such reasoning is that there are many more ways of being not-red than there are of being red, so absence any evidence concerning color, one should probably conclude that the shirt is not red.[74]

Although there are important questions about just how to interpret it, the principle of indifference might still be useful. Suppose that one randomly pulls 100 red balls out of a sack that one knows contains about 1,000 balls. At this point, it would, presumably, be rational to believe that most of the balls in the sack are red. It is perfectly *conceivable* that 90 percent of the balls in the sack are some other color, but unless the act of selecting a ball somehow partially determines the color of the ball (again something that is perfectly *conceivable*), we would reason that were the balls *not* mostly red we would have picked at least one ball that wasn't red in our first 100 picks.

---

[74] There are also interesting puzzles that arise concerning attempts to apply the principle of indifference. It would take us too far afield, however, to explore those puzzles in any sort of detail here. But consider the following (a variation of *Bertrand's* paradox): Suppose you know that a given figure is a square and that its sides are somewhere between 2" and 4" long (you know nothing else). At first blush, you might be inclined to supposed that it is equally likely that the sides are between 2" and 3", and that they are between 3" and 4". But it is also true, of course, that given the information one can infer that the area of the square is somewhere between 4" and 16". So just thinking about *areas* one might think that it is equally like that the area is between 4" and 10" as that it is between 10" and 16". But one can't consistently hold both the view about the likelihood concerning the length of the sides and the likelihood concerning the areas.

There is an obviously correct principle of *deductively valid* reasoning called *modus tollens*. I suspect that it might be the most commonly used principle of reasoning in philosophy. The principle asserts that IF 1) if P then Q and 2) not-Q, THEN not-P. Philosophers often rely on this principle to reject a theory by drawing from it some obviously unacceptable (false) consequence.[75] It is tempting to think that there is an analogous principle of nondeductive reasoning: IF 1) If P makes probable Q and 2) not-Q, THEN probably not-P. So, for example, a great many people concluded immediately that COVID-19 is a virus that escaped from the lab in Wuhan that was studying coronaviruses. If the virus were a natural mutation of viruses spread among animals in the wild then it is exceedingly unlikely that it would have begun in just the place where such viruses are studied. It did begin there, so it probably wasn't a natural occurrence. When reasoning nondeductively, however, it is critical that one keeps in mind the fact that even if P makes probable Q, it doesn't follow that P together with anything else X makes probable Q. The fact that I seem to remember putting my keys on my desk might make probable that I put the keys on my desk. But when I add to that apparent memory the fact that I look carefully on my desk and see no keys, my new evidence no longer makes probable that the keys are there.[76] In the same way, one *might* have additional evidence that suggests that the COVID-19 pandemic wasn't caused by a lab leak.

Still, if I don't know anything else that bears on the likelihood of P and I know that P makes probable Q, then when I discover not-Q doesn't that give me reason to believe that not-P? After all, if my total body of evidence suggests that P makes probable Q, then doesn't my total body of evidence also *justify* me in believing that if P is true then Q is true. But then when I discover not-Q, I can employ the *uncontroversial* rule of *modus tollens* to conclude that not-P. As we noted earlier, one's justification for believing the conclusion of some argument based (solely) on the premises of that argument is never any stronger than the justification one has for believing the premises. Still, that doesn't affect the claim just made about what I would be justified in believing.[77]

---

[75] And the philosopher Karl Popper (1959) famously suggested that the use of *modus tollens* characterizes the approach of scientists to theory confirmation. The basic idea is that scientists construct theories that have observational consequences. The theory continues to be accepted until one can't make one of the observations that the theory implies one should have been able to make. At that point, the theory needs to be abandoned or modified.

[76] That is an important difference between the relation of making probable and the relation of entailment. From the fact that P entails Q (the fact that it is impossible for P to be true while Q is false) it does follow that P conjoined with anything else E entails Q. From the fact that P makes probable Q it doesn't follow that P conjoined with anything else E makes probable Q.

[77] One might even argue that a well-known piece of fallacious reasoning isn't as bad as philosophers make it out to be. One cannot validly infer from 1) if P then Q and 2) Q, that 3) P. That is called the fallacy of affirming the consequent. But often in ordinary conversation when we claim that if

One way of seeing how such reasoning is legitimate is to reflect on another principle that might be plausibly included in the foundations of knowledge, Bayes Theorem:

The probability of A given B = The (prior) probability of B given A multiplied by the (prior) probability of A, the product of which is divided by the (prior) probability of B

There are all sorts of questions that arise concerning the critical notion of *prior* probabilities. Some Bayesians seem to interpret these "subjectively," where the prior probabilities just represent the degree of confidence one has that the propositions in questions are true. In this context, I'll presuppose that the priors represent the probabilities relative to one's total body of evidence prior to learning that B. And **one** way of getting prior probabilities is to employ something like a principle of indifference. If we do that using our example above of random drawing of balls, the theorem will give us a very high probability that at least most of the balls are red given the 100 red balls that we drew. After all, knowing nothing about the color of the balls in the sack (although, let us suppose, knowing that there are balls that have some color or other), we would treat the probability of all of the balls being red, all of the balls being blue, etc., all but one of the balls being red, all but one of the balls being blue, etc., as having the same probability. So the prior probability of *all* of the balls being red is *tiny*.[78] But the probability of getting 100 red balls given that all of the balls are red is 1 (or given that almost all of the balls are red is very high). The prior probability of selecting 100 red balls (given the lack of knowledge we are presupposing) is also very low.

It is tempting to think that one might be able to employ a similar sort of reasoning to reconstruct inductive reasoning. We have seen a lot of ravens almost all of which were black. Unless it were true that most ravens are black (we think), we would have run into more nonblack ravens. So most ravens are black. The priors this time, however, are even more difficult to calculate given that we are dealing with a class of ravens that *might* be infinitely large.[79]

P then Q we are leading the person with whom we are communicating to understand that if not-P then not-Q. For example, when a parent tells a child that if they clean up their room they can watch TV for another hour, the child will typically suppose that the parent is also suggesting that if they *don't* clean up their room, they *won't* get to which that other hour of television. But from 1) if not-P then not-Q and 2) Q one *can* legitimately infer not-P. The fallacy of affirming the consequent, might also involve nothing more problematic that conversational assumptions that people often quite naturally make. For more on what Grice called "conversational implication"; see Grice (1975).

[78] It is not easy to come up with an exact probability, given the problem of how to partition classes. The first thing one would need to divide up the color spectrum giving equal "width" to the red band, the blue band, the yellow band, and so on.

[79] Remember that we are talking about *all* ravens *everywhere* past, present, and future.

4.3 Internalist Constraints on Discovering the Truth of Epistemic Principles

We noted earlier that inferential externalists deny the need to have justification for accepting an epistemic principle in order to employ effectively reasoning sanctioned by such a principle. And if pressed on how one might justify a belief in such principles, the externalist has a view that allows one to use the very principle at issue to certify its own legitimacy. So, for example, on a reliabilist's view of justification, *if* reliance on apparent memory and inductive reasoning *are* both reliable ways of forming beliefs about the past, *then* one could get justification for believing that memory is reliable by relying on apparent memory to get an inductive "track record" of successful reliance on apparent memory to establish the reliability of memory.

Internalist are typically outraged at the suggestion that one can use a kind of reasoning to certify the legitimacy of relying on that sort of reasoning. But it is worth acknowledging that one isn't *guaranteed* smooth sailing just because one employs a kind of reasoning to establish its reliability. Some of you might be familiar with the "magic" eight-ball with which children sometimes play. You ask the eight-ball a question and an answer floats to a transparent part of the ball. The answers range from "Yes," "Definitely," "Without Doubt" to "Maybe," or "Ask me again," all the way to "No," or "Definitely not." When challenged to establish the reliability of eight-ball "reasoning," a practitioner might get the bright idea of asking the eight-ball: "Are your answers a reliable guide to reality?" An internalist might immediately cry foul. Wait. You can't *use* eight-ball reasoning to establish the reliability of eight-ball reasoning! But the futility of such an attempt isn't really *quite* that obvious. To be sure, if the ball says "Yes," in answer to a question about its reliability, the skeptic will be unconvinced. But suppose we agree to *repeatedly* ask the question, and the answer always comes up "Yes." And for added support the eight-ball reasoner, repeatedly ask the question are you unreliable, and the eight-ball keeps answering "Definitely, not!" We further test the eight-ball by asking other sorts of questions such as "Is snow white?" and "Is the sky blue?," and the eight-ball keeps getting those answers right. Something is up, right? You are probably going to start taking eight-ball reasoning seriously.

Of course, in the situation discussed above, we are supposing that we have an *independent* way of checking the accuracy of some of the eight-ball's claims. But again, the point I want to stress here is that things don't need to go well for the eight-ball reasoner trying to use the eight-ball to certify its reliability. Suppose the eight-ball reasoner asks the eight-ball "Are you reliable?" and eight-ball answers "Definitely not!?" That's not good for the eight-ball reasoner! And suppose the eight-ball reasoner continues to ask the question, and the eight-ball continues to deny its own reliability. Eight-ball reasoning has turned on itself. It presumably won't do for the eight-ball reasoner to dismiss the eight-ball's denial of its reliability by pointing out that if it is right and it is unreliable, then we can't conclude on the basis of its "conclusions" that it is unreliable. There is still a problem that needs to be solved before continuing to rely on the eight-ball. And things aren't much better for the adherent of eight-ball reasoning if the repeated answers to the question about reliability see-saws back and forth between "Yes" and "No."

There is a sense in which some of the actual ways in which people rely on various sorts of input to reach conclusions can also turn on themselves. We might try to rely on apparent memory to inductively justify the reliability of memory. Again, the internalist will cry foul. But it is worth noting that the attempt to use apparent memory to justify one's belief about its reliability *need* not succeed. I might seem to remember having put the keys on my mantlepiece, and *also* seem to remember not finding them there. I might seem to remember having had an excruciating headache yesterday, but also seem to remember reading in my diary that yesterday I had no pain whatsoever. Memory can turn on itself. Indeed, I imagine that one of the most frightening features of the early stages of devastating Alzheimer's disease is that period when the victim realizes, *relying* on apparent memory, that they can't rely on apparent memory. So the fact that things go well when they might not have gone well is at least *some* reason for relying on apparent memory. It's not that we can't easily imagine some skeptical scenario being true. We might be fooled by evil demons or nefarious evil scientists who have implanted in us nonveridical apparent memory. But it is still an epistemic mark in favor of reliance on apparent memory that memory does not usually turn on itself in the way described above.

4.4 Does Traditional Foundationalism "Over-Intellectualize" Requirements for Justified Belief?

We have been trying to find ways to build on a traditional foundationalist's foundations, and we have been trying to do so in an intellectually satisfying way. Even if we convince ourselves that the project isn't futile, many would claim that it is wildly implausible as an account of any sort of reasoning in which ordinary people *actually* engage. Five-year-old children know when their mother is angry at them. They know all sorts of truths about their past and their surroundings. Their beliefs about such matters are perfectly rational. But they haven't been contemplating the premises of inductive arguments or reasoning to the best explanation, neither have they been employing a principle of indifference in an attempt to discover prior probabilities that might be of use in Bayesian reasoning. As we noted earlier, this sort of consideration contributes to the attraction that externalist epistemologies have for many determined to avoid what they take to be implausible skepticism.

Internalists might be able to offer an olive branch when it comes to the worry about over-intellectualizing requirements for knowledge and justified belief. When we first worried about externalists "changing" the subject of traditional philosophical concern with their externalist analyses of knowledge and justified belief, perhaps we should have emphasized "philosophical." We worried that defining foundational justification in terms of the causal history of a belief or the reliability of the process leading to a belief would make justification something that does nothing to satisfy *philosophical* curiosity – would make justification irrelevant to the search for intellectual assurance. But most people aren't philosophers. They may not even raise questions about the justification available to support a belief, let alone try to answer the questions in a way that would provide assurance.

4.4.1 Ideal Justification

Perhaps we might go some way to bridge the divide between traditional foundationalism and newer externalist accounts of foundational justification by admitting that the traditional foundationlist seeks justification that would give the intellectually curious philosopher a certain sort of *philosophically* satisfying assurance. We could call that justification *ideal* justification. And we might also recognize that there are derivative concepts of knowledge and justified belief that fall short of ideal justification.

4.4.2 Derivative Concepts of Justification

We noted earlier that most externalists reject the claim that to move by inference beyond foundations one needs some sort of access to the legitimacy of the relevant inference. Without such access we might seem to lack the kind of justification a philosopher seeks. But, inspired by Hume, we might also acknowledge that even lacking such awareness, we *might* have evolved in such a way that we are *caused* to believe propositions by experiences that are truth-makers for propositions that might make probable the truths we end up believing.

We noted earlier that traditional foundationalists are often criticized for implying that ordinary people engage in the kind of introspection that involves forming beliefs about the ever-changing subjective character of experience. We

noted that becoming aware of experience *in this way* might be better thought of
as a skill that can be learned, the kind of skill that someone learning how to paint
might acquire. But you will also recall that we distinguished between *having* an
experience, being *aware* of an experience, and forming a *belief* that one has an
experience. Hume famously argued that it is in principle possible for anything to
cause anything else. Whether or not once accepts a principle that general, it
certainly seems possible that we have evolved in such a way that experience, or,
perhaps more plausibly, patterns of experiences might cause us to form beliefs
about the world around us. Or, more modestly still, one might suppose that
patterns of experiences cause us to form various *expectations* about future
experiences. The expectations might consist of little more than surprise that
would occur were certain experiences not to occur. The experiences that cause
beliefs and expectations are, of course, features of the world that would make
true propositions describing them, and would do so even if the person who has
those experiences formed none of the relevant beliefs.

Without understanding how the relevant propositions describing experiences
make probable truths about the physical world, one gets no *philosophical*
understanding of a sort that would provide assurance. Without that understanding, one lacks ideal justification (and ideal knowledge that might be tied to that
justification). But *if* the experiences make true propositions that do constitute
legitimate evidence for beliefs about the existence of the physical objects, that
might be viewed as a *kind* of justification that falls short of the ideal.

I suggested that if a belief is caused by facts that make propositions true when
those propositions are relevant evidence for the truth of what is believed, that
might generate a kind of derivative justification that falls short of an ideal. But
one might also recognize still more "degenerate" forms of justification. So
I have argued elsewhere (Fumerton1985) that it is only *patterns* of experiences
together with hypothesis about what constitutes a plausible causal explanation
of those patterns that would yield plausible evidence for commonsense beliefs.
And even that cryptic claim is plausible only if we understand the content of
claims about the physical world in terms of metaphysically neutral claims about
potential causes of patterns of experience. Perhaps we have complex background metaphysical and epistemological beliefs that lurk beneath consciousness that would do the relevant epistemic work, but until those background
beliefs are brought to the fore of consciousness, they would again do nothing to
answer philosophical questions in a philosophically satisfying way.

To satisfy philosophical curiosity, one needs to explore thoroughly *metaphysical* questions that would take us far beyond the scope of this work.
Epistemological solutions to the problem of perception, for example, will
require exploring *conceptual* connections between our thought about the

physical world and our thought about appearance. Some philosophers have argued that one can "translate" talk about the physical world into talk about connections among sensations. Others have argued that we can "translate" talk about physical objects into talk about the causes of sensations and connections about sensations (where we attribute no intrinsic character to these causes). It is an understatement to suggest that both views are highly controversial. As I argued earlier, foundational knowledge of necessary truths would require reaching conclusions about the *truth-makers* for necessary truths. To argue that knowledge of necessary truths is based on acquaintance with universals and relations among them one would need to argue for the metaphysical position that there *are* universals and that relations among them make true necessary truths. Alternatively, to argue that knowledge of necessary truths is based on acquaintance with relations among thoughts, one would need a *metaphysical* account of the nature of thought and one would need to explain how relations among thoughts can make true paradigmatic necessary truths. I've argued elsewhere for metaphysical positions that bear on these epistemological problems (Fumerton 2002). Here I'm pointing out only that without this sort of metaphysical investigation one can't reach philosophically satisfying conclusions about how truths about subjective experience can make probable truths about the physical world, or how awareness of universals or thoughts can justify beliefs about necessary truths.[80]

[80] I would like to thank Michael Huemer for the helpful comments and suggestions he made on an earlier draft of this Element.

References

Armstrong, David. 1973. *Belief, Truth, and Knowledge*. London: Cambridge University Press.

Audi, Robert. 1998. *Epistemology*. New York and London: Routledge.

Bergmann, Michael, 2006. *Justification without Awareness*. Oxford: Oxford University Press.

Berkeley, George. 1954. *Three Dialogues Between Hylas and Philonous*, ed. Colin M. Turbayne. Indianapolis, IN: Bobbs-Merrill.

BonJour, Laurence. 1985. *The Structure of Empirical Knowledge*. Cambridge: Harvard University Press.

and Sosa, Ernest. 2003. *Epistemic Justification*. Oxford: Blackwell.

Broad, C. D. 1923. *Scientific Thought*. London: Routledge & Kegan Paul.

1938. *An Investigation of McTaggart's Philosophy*, Vol. II, Part I. Cambridge: Cambridge University Press.

Butchvarov, Panayot. 1970. *The Concept of Knowledge*. Evanston, IL: Northwestern University Press.

Carroll, Lewis. 1895. "What the Tortoise Said to Achilles." *Mind* (4) 278–80.

Chisholm, R. M. 1966. *Theory of Knowledge*, 1st ed. Englewood Cliffs, NJ: Prentice-Hall.

1989. *Theory of Knowledge*, 3rd ed. Englewood Cliffs, NJ: Prentice-Hall.

Cohen, Stewart. 1999. "Contextualism, Skepticism, and the Structure of Reasons." *Philosophical Perspectives* (13) 57–89.

2002. "Basic Knowledge and the Problem of Easy Knowledge." *Philosophy and Phenomenological Research* (65) 309–29.

Cole, Peter, and Jerry L. Morgan (eds.). 1975. *Syntax and Semantics, 3: Speech Acts*. New York: Academic Press.

Conee, Earl, and Feldman, Richard. 1998. "The Generality Problem for Reliabilism." *Philosophical Studies* (89) 1–29.

DePaul, Michael (ed.). 2001. *Resurrecting Old-Fashioned Foundationalism*. Lanham, MD: Rowman & Littlefield.

Descartes, Rene. 1960. *Discourse on Method and Meditations*, trans. Laurence J. Lafleur. Indianapolis, IL: Bobbs-Merrill.

Eddington, Arthur. 1929. *The Nature of the Physical World*. New York: Macmillan.

Fales, Evan. 1996. *A Defense of the Given*. Lanham, MD: Rowman & Littlefield.

Fantl, Jeremy, and Matthew McGrath. 2002. "Evidence, Pragmatics and Justification." *Philosophical Review* (111) 67–94.

Firth, Roderick. 1959. "Chisholm and the Ethics of Belief." *Philosophical Review* (68) (4) 493–506.

Foley, Richard. 1979. "Justified Inconsistent Beliefs." *American Philosophical Quarterly* (16) 247–58.

Fumerton, Richard. 1985. *Metaphysical and Epistemological Problems of Perception.* Lincoln and London: University of Nebraska Press.

1989. "Russelling Causal Theories of Reference." In *Rereading Russell*, eds. Wade Savage and C. Anthony Anderson. Minneapolis: University of Minnesota Press, 108–18.

1994. "The Incoherence of Coherence Theories," *Journal of Philosophical Research* (XIX) 89–102.

1996. *Metaepistemology and Skepticism.* Boston, MA: Rowman & Littlefield.

2002. *Realism and the Correspondence Theory of Truth.* Lanham, MD: Rowman & Littlefield.

2014. "Infinitism." In *Ad Infinitum: New Essays on Epistemological Infinitism*, eds. John Turri and Peter Klein. Oxford: Oxford University Press, 75–86.

2016. "Prospects for Traditional Internalism." In *Intellectual Assurance: Essays on Traditional Epistemic Internalism*, eds. Michael Bergmann and Brett Coppenger. Oxford: Oxford University Press, 239–57.

2018. "Inferential Internalism and the Problem of Unconscious Inference." In *The Mystery of Skepticism – New Explorations*, eds. Kevin McCain and Ted Poston. Leiden: Brill, 176–86.

Gettier, Edmund. 1963. "Is Justified True Belief Knowledge?" *Analysis* (23) 121–3.

Ginet, Carl. 1975. *Knowledge, Perception and Memory.* Dordrecht: Reidel Publishing.

Goldman, Alvin. 1967. "A Causal Theory of Knowing." *Journal of Philosophy* (64) 355–72.

1979. "What is Justified Belief?" In *Justification and Knowledge*, ed. George Pappas. Dordrecht: Reidel, 1–23.

1986. *Epistemology and Cognition.* Cambridge: Harvard University Press.

1988. "Strong and Weak Justification." In *Philosophical Perspectives 2: Epistemology*, ed. James Toberlin. Atascadero, CA: Ridgeview Publishing Co., 51–69.

1999. "Internalism Exposed." *Journal of Philosophy* 96 (6) 271–93.

Grice, Paul. 1975. "Logic and Conversation." In *Syntax and Semantics, 3: Speech Acts*, eds. Peter Cole and Jerry L. Morgan . New York: Academic Press,41–58.

Haack, Susan. 1995. *Evidence and Inquiry: Towards Reconstruction in Epistemology.* Oxford: Blackwell.

Hawthorne, John. 2003. *Knowledge and Lotteries.* Oxford: Clarendon Press.

Huemer, Mike. 2001. *Skepticism and the Veil of Perception.* Lanham, MD: Rowman & Littlefield.

    2002. "Fumerton's Principle of Inferential Justification." *Journal of Philosophical Research* (27) 329–40.

    2019. "Finite Minds." In *Themes From Klein* eds. Cherie Braden, Rodrigo Borges, and Branden Fitelson. Branden: Springer Verlag, 171–87.

Hume, David. 1888. *A Treatise of Human Nature*, ed. L. A. Selby-Bigge. London: Oxford University Press.

James, William. 1890. *The Principles of Psychology.* New York: Dover.

Keynes, John. 1921. *A Treatise on Probability.* London: Macmillan.

Klein, Peter. 1998. "Foundationalism and the Infinite Regress of Reasons." *Philosophy and Phenomenological Research* (58) (4) 919–25.

    1999. "Human Knowledge and the Infinite Regress of Reasons." In *Philosophical Perspectives 13: Epistemology*, ed. James Tomberlin. Oxford: Blackwell, 297–325.

    2014. "Reasons, Reasoning and Knowledge: A Proposed Rapprochement between Infinitism and Foundationalism." In *Ad Infinitum: New Essays on Epistemological Infinitism*, eds. P. Klein and J. Turri Oxford: Oxford University Press, 105–24.

Kripke, Saul. 1980. *Naming and Necessity.* Cambridge: Harvard University Press.

Lewis, David. 1996. "Elusive Knowledge." *Australasian Journal of Philosophy* (5) 49–67.

Littlejohn, Clayton. Forthcoming. "A Plea for Epistemic Excuses." In *The New Evil Demon*, ed. Julien Dutant. London: Oxford University Press.

McGrew, Timothy, 1995. *The Foundations of Knowledge.* Lanham, MA: Littlefield Addams.

Mill, John Stuart. 1963–91. *The Collected Works of John Stuart Mill*, ed. John M. Robson. Toronto: University of Toronto Press.

Moore, G. E. 1959. "A Defence of Common Sense". In *Philosophical Papers* . London: Allen & Unwin, 32–5.

Peirce, C. S. 1938. *Collected Papers*, eds. C. Hartshorne and P. Weis. Cambridge: Harvard University Press.

Plantinga, Alvan. 1992. "Justification in the 20th Century." In *Philosophical Issues 2: Rationality in Epistemology*, ed. Enrique Villanueva. Atascadero, CA : Ridgeview Publishing Co., 43–78.

1993. *Warrant and Proper Function*. New York: Oxford University Press.

2000. *Warranted Christian Belief*. New York: Oxford University Press.

Popper, Karl. 1959. *The Logic of Scientific Discovery*. London: Hutchinson.

Price, H. H. 1932. *Perception*. London: Methuen & Co. Ltd.

Quine, W. V. O. 1969. "Epistemology Naturalized." In *Ontological Relativity and Other Essays*. New York: Columbia University Press.

Reid, Thomas. 1764/1997. *An Inquiry into the Human Mind on the Principles of Common Sense*, ed. Derek R. Brookes. University Park: Pennsylvania State University Press.

Russell, Bertrand. 1940. *An Inquiry Into Meaning and Truth*. New York: W. W. Norton and Co., 14–15.

1948. *Human Knowledge: Its Scope and Limits*. New York: Simon & Schuster.

1959. *The Problems of Philosophy*. Oxford: Oxford University Press.

Sellars, Wilfred. 1963. *Science, Perception and Reality*. London: Routledge & Kegan Paul.

Shope, Robert. 1978. "The Conditional Fallacy in Contemporary Philosophy." *Journal of Philosophy* (75) 397–413.

Sosa, Ernest. 1991. *Knowledge in Perspective*. Cambridge: Cambridge University Press.

and Lawrence BonJour. 2003. *Foundations vs Virtues*. London: Blackwell.

Ushenko, Andrew Paul. 1937. *The Philosophy of Relativity*. London: Allen & Unwin.

Vos Savant, Marilyn, 1990. "Ask Marilyn" column in *Parade Magazine*, September 9, p. 16.

Williamson, Timothy. 2000. *Knowledge and its Limits*. Oxford: Oxford University Press.

Forthcoming. "Justification, Excuses and Sceptical Scenarios." In *The New Evil Demon*, ed. Julien Dutant. London: Oxford University Press.

Wilson, Jennifer. 2004. "Rethinking the *A Priori/A Posteriori* Distinction." Unpublished.

Cambridge Elements ≡

Epistemology

Stephen Hetherington

University of New South Wales, Sydney

Stephen Hetherington is Professor Emeritus of Philosophy at the University of New South Wales, Sydney.

He is the author of numerous books, including *Knowledge and the Gettier Problem* (Cambridge University Press, 2016) and *What Is Epistemology?* (Polity, 2019), and is the editor of several others, including *Knowledge in Contemporary Epistemology* (with Markos Valaris: Bloomsbury, 2019) and *What the Ancients Offer to Contemporary Epistemology* (with Nicholas D. Smith: Routledge, 2020). He was the Editor-in-Chief of the *Australasian Journal of Philosophy* from 2013 until 2022.

About the Series

This Elements series seeks to cover all aspects of a rapidly evolving field including emerging and evolving topics such as these: fallibilism; knowing-how; self-knowledge; knowledge of morality; knowledge and injustice; formal epistemology; knowledge and religion; scientific knowledge; collective epistemology; applied epistemology; virtue epistemology; wisdom. The series will demonstrate the liveliness and diversity of the field, pointing also to new areas of investigation.

Cambridge Elements ≡

Epistemology

Elements in the Series

The Epistemic Consequences of Paradox
Bryan Frances

Foundationalism
Richard Fumerton

A full series listing is available at: www.cambridge.org/EEPI

Printed in the United States
by Baker & Taylor Publisher Services